A PRIMER ON DIVINE REVELATION
Scripture and Tradition

Dwight P. Campbell

A PRIMER ON DIVINE REVELATION
Scripture and Tradition

Scepter Publishers Inc.
Princeton, New Jersey

Midwest Theological Forum
Chicago

This edition of
A PRIMER ON DIVINE REVELATION
Scripture and Tradition
is published by

SCEPTER PUBLISHERS, INC.
P.O. Box 1270
Princeton, New Jersey 08542
email: general@scepterpub.org

and

MIDWEST THEOLOGICAL FORUM
712 South Loomis St.
Chicago, Illinois 60607
Tel. 312-421-8135 Fax 312-421-8129
email: mail@mwtf.org

First Edition 1998

Nihil Obstat: Rev. Msgr. Steven P. Rohlfs, S.T.D.
Censor Librorum

Imprimatur: +Most Rev. John J. Myers, S.T.L., J.C.D.
Bishop of Peoria

ISBN 1-890177-06-7

Cover: "Christ Pantocrator." Icon in encaustic wax, first half of the 6th century. Monastery of St. Catharine, Sinai.

DEDICATION

To Mary, our Queen and our Mother,
through whom Jesus Christ,
the fullness of Divine Revelation,
has come to us

For the word of God is a light to the mind and a fire to the will. It enables man to know God and to love Him. And for the interior man who lives by the Spirit of God through grace, it is bread and water, but a bread sweeter than honey and the honeycomb, a water better than wine and milk. For the soul it is a spiritual treasure of merits yielding an abundance of gold and precious stones. Against the hardness of a heart that persists in wrongdoing, it acts as a hammer. Against the world, the flesh and the devil it serves as a sword that destroys all sin.

St. Lawrence of Brindisi
Liturgy of the Hours, Vol. III, p. 1542

CONTENTS

Foreword

I was recently asked by Fr. Joseph Fessio S.J. of Ignatius Press to write a blurb of appreciation for Joseph Cardinal Ratzinger's recently translated work, *Gospel, Catechesis, Catechism: Sidelights on the Catechism of the Catholic Church.*

After reading Fr. Dwight P. Campbell's *A PRIMER ON DIVINE REVELATION*, I must admit that this latter work finds continual resonance in the work of Joseph Cardinal Ratzinger, the Prefect of the Sacred Congregation for the Doctrine of the Faith.

The cardinal quotes the great Jewish scholar Jacob Neusner, who has vigorously opposed contemporary reconstruction and devaluation of the Gospels. The rabbi declares: "I write for believing Christians and faithful Jews; for them, Jesus is known through the Gospels." Cardinal Ratzinger observes that contemporary biblical scholarship has frequently resulted in the dissolution of the biblical witness about Jesus into a variety of fabricated personae, leading to a frightfully impoverished image of Jesus, thereby rendering any living relationship with him almost impossible. His Eminence then takes on one of the authors carefully reviewed by Father Campbell and observes, "What remains of the image of Jesus is often terribly meager .... Can acquaintance with a marginal Jew from a very distant past be "gospel, glad tidings"?

Father Campbell, in line with the suggestions of Cardinal Ratzinger, demonstrates how the *Catechism* masterfully assists us in encountering the Jesus of History. The time has come for an awareness that hypotheses or theories set forth by contemporary scriptural exegetes, whether Catholic or Protestant, should not be presented as certitudes.

In a talk delivered recently in Novara, Italy, to a group of seminary rectors and spiritual directors during a seminar, Christoph Cardinal Schönborn, Archbishop of Vienna, remarked:

"The best formation comes when we become familiar with Christ, when the Holy Spirit leads our thoughts and our heart, and grace transforms our habits. Then we judge theologically, not only by reason, but by the heart. We make a judgment, not only through intellectual knowledge but through a spiritual intuition about what is right and what is wrong. It is vital during theological studies, then, to read the saints. Isn't it true that only great intellectual capacity joined with true sanctity makes the true theologian?"

As Cardinal Ratzinger pointedly observes:

"When I ask myself why our churches are emptying out, why our faith is trickling away, I would answer that one of the chief reasons is the evacuation of the figure of Jesus, coupled with the deistic conception of God. The more or less romantic ersatz Jesus currently being offered is not enough. He lacks reality; he is too far away. But the Jesus of the Gospels, whom we come to know again in the *Catechism*, is present because he is the Son and accessible to me because he is man. His human history is never merely a thing of the past; all of it is preserved in him and in the communion of his disciples as a thing of the present that still touches me today."

It is my fervent hope that Father Campbell's *A PRIMER ON DIVINE REVELATION* will enkindle in all who read it such a personal relationship with Jesus as is found in Cardinal Ratzinger's *Gospel, Catechesis, Catechism*, and echoed so well by the above statement of Christoph Cardinal Schönborn.

Rev. Msgr. Michael J. Wrenn, K.H.S., M.A., M.S., D.H.L.
Pastor of St. John the Evangelist Church
New York City

Preface

At the Last Supper, Jesus Christ prayed to the Father for unity among the future members of his Mystical Body, the Church: "I pray not only for them, but also *for those who will believe in me through their word, so that they may all be one,* as you, Father, are in me and I in you. . . . And I have given them the glory you gave me, so that they may be one, as we are one, I in them and you in me, that they may be brought to perfection as one. . . ." (*Jn* 17:20–23; emphasis added).

As Jesus makes clear in this passage, unity in the Church was to come through belief in the divinely revealed word that his Apostles and their successors in office would teach: the Gospel, or Good News, of salvation. Unfortunately, the unity for which Jesus prayed (*"Ut unum sint"*) has been broken over the centuries through separations from the Church and its supreme authority, the pope, who is the Vicar of Christ on earth. Non-Catholic Christians do not share completely our understanding of the articles of the Faith, of the sacraments, and of the means to salvation. Even among Catholics, especially in the years following the Second Vatican Council, divisions have resulted, principally from a failure to submit in obedience of Faith to the divinely revealed Word, as handed down through the successors to the Apostles, on matters of faith and morals.

I am personally convinced that if people correctly understood Divine Revelation and how the teaching of Christ, first deposited with the Apostles, is passed down to us, then the unity for which Jesus prayed, and for which he sacrificed his life on the Cross, would become a reality. The pope and bishops at the Second Vatican Council no doubt had this end in mind when writing *Dei Verbum* ("Dogmatic Constitution on Divine Revelation"), which beautifully sets forth, in a most comprehensive manner, "the true doctrine on Divine Revelation and its transmission."

"For," as the Preface to *Dei Verbum* goes on to say, the Council "wants the whole world to hear the summons to salvation, so that through hearing it may believe, through belief it may hope, through hope it may come to love."

It is toward this end—the fostering of a correct understanding of Divine Revelation, as found in both Sacred Tradition and Sacred Scripture—that I have written *A PRIMER ON DIVINE REVELATION*. The *PRIMER* systematically goes through each article of *Dei Verbum* and explains, by use of questions and answers, the rich teaching found in this dogmatic constitution. It will help the reader understand precisely why we, as Catholics, believe what we believe: that we do so because the truths of our Faith have been revealed by God himself, through Jesus Christ and the Holy Spirit; and have been passed down to us through Sacred Tradition (the revealed Word of God in the teachings of the Church) and Sacred Scripture (the revealed Word of God in written form).

In particular, I think the reader will find most helpful the explanations of the relationship between Sacred Tradition, Sacred Scripture, and the Magisterium in the transmission of Divine Revelation; the meaning of divine inspiration and its interpretation; and the teaching of the Church regarding the authorship and historicity of the four Gospels, which includes a refutation of modern errors in this area. To further assist the reader I have cross-referred the teachings of *Dei Verbum* to the *Catechism of the Catholic Church (CCC)*.

My hope is that the reader may gain a deeper understanding and appreciation for the divinely revealed Word of God, deposited by Jesus Christ with the Apostles and passed down to us today through Tradition and Scripture; and that through a true understanding of the revealed Word of God, the unity for which Christ prayed may be realized.

Rev. Fr. Dwight P. Campbell
St. Thomas Church, Philo, Illinois

Chapter I
Divine Revelation Itself

1. **What is the purpose of the Dogmatic Constitution on Divine Revelation** *(Dei Verbum)*?

   As stated in Art. 1, the Preface of *Dei Verbum*, "Following, then, in the steps of the Councils of Trent and Vatican I, this Synod wishes to set forth the true doctrine on Divine Revelation and its transmission. For it wants the whole world to hear the summons of salvation, so that through hearing it may believe, through belief it may hope, through hope it may come to love."

2. **What is meant when the Church speaks of the "mystery of [God's] will"?**

   It means that God is a mystery, and his loving plan of salvation is likewise a mystery: "In all his wisdom and insight, [God] has made known to us the mystery of his will. . . ." *(Eph* 1:9).

3. **What is a (supernatural) mystery?**

   A supernatural mystery is a divinely revealed truth that cannot be known by the human mind prior to its being revealed by God (e.g., the mystery of the Blessed Trinity, three divine persons in one God; or the mystery of the Incarnation, the Son of God uniting to himself a human nature while remaining God) and that still cannot be fully understood by man even after it has been revealed.

4. **What is Divine Revelation?**

   Divine Revelation is God revealing himself and his will to us, so that through Christ and in the Holy Spirit we may come to the Father and share in the divine nature. Divine Revelation is a *communication* by God to us, to establish with us a personal relationship and enable us to become children of God. Simply put, Divine Revelation is God revealing himself and his plan of salvation to us.

5. **How do we go to the Father in heaven?**

    We go to our Father in heaven through Jesus, his Son, in the Holy Spirit: " . . . for through [Christ] we both have access in one Spirit to the Father" (*Eph* 2:18).

6. **The Church and Scripture teach that through Jesus and in the Holy Spirit we share in the "divine nature": "[Christ] has bestowed on us the precious and very great promises, so that through them you may come to share in the divine nature. . . ." (2 *Pet* 1:4). What does this mean?**

    We are conceived and born into this world with a human nature. Our goal is to be with the Father in heaven, where we will share in God's own divine nature, which means we will share in God's own divine life.

7. **When do we first share in the divine nature, God's own divine life?**

    At Baptism, when we are "born again" by water and the Spirit, and begin to share in God's own divine life: "Jesus answered [Nicodemus], 'Amen, Amen, I say to you, no one can enter the Kingdom of God without being born of water and Spirit" (*Jn* 3:5). In heaven we will share fully in the divine nature, God's own divine life.

8. **What does it mean to say that God "provides men with constant evidence of himself in created realities"?**

    Creation, being a reflection of the Creator, proclaims the existence and attributes of God. (*See* Art. 6 of *Dei Verbum*)

9. **When and to whom did God first reveal to man his plan of redemption and salvation?**

    In the beginning, to our first parents, Adam and Eve, after their fall from God's grace. God promised salvation to the human race when he said to the devil, represented by the serpent: "I will put enmity between you and the woman, between your offspring and hers; he will strike at your head, while you strike at his heel" (*Gen* 3:15). This verse is commonly known as the *Protoevangelium*, or *Protogospel*; i.e., the First Good News. Sacred Tradition holds that the "woman" refers primarily to the Blessed Virgin Mary, and her offspring refers to Jesus Christ.

It should be noted that in the original Hebrew text, the word that is translated as "he" in the above text from Genesis is actually a neuter pronoun, which is properly translated as "it." The Septuagint[1] (Greek) translation uses the masculine: *autos*—"he will strike at [or crush] your head"—a Messianic interpretation, referring to Christ.

The Latin Vulgate (or "common") translation done by St. Jerome in the 4th century A.D. uses the feminine: *ipsa*—"she will strike at [or crush] your head"—an interpretation referring to Mary; hence, some later translations of the Bible into the vernacular based on the Latin Vulgate (e.g., the English Douay-Rheims) translate the above verse in this manner. In a secondary sense Mary, by reason of her unique cooperation in the Incarnation (when the Son of God took a human nature in her womb) and the Redemption (when she stood at the foot of the Cross), can also be said to strike at or crush Satan's head. This is why statues and works of art portraying Mary as "Our Lady of Grace" show her standing atop the world with her foot over the serpent's head.

The Latin Neovulgate opts for the neuter: *ipsum*—"it." More recent translations (e.g., the *New American Bible*) translate the Hebrew pronoun as "he."

In his general audience of Jan. 24, 1996, Pope John Paul II explains why: "Exegetes now agree in recognizing that the text of Genesis, according to the original Hebrew, does not attribute action against the serpent directly to the woman, but to her offspring. Nevertheless, the text gives great prominence to the role she will play in the struggle against the tempter: In fact, the one who defeats the serpent will be her offspring."[2]

10. To whom else did God reveal his plan of salvation in the Old Testament?

To Abraham, Moses, and the Prophets.

---

1. The Septuagint is the Greek translation of the Old Testament first done by 72 Hebrew Scripture scholars near the end of the 4th century B.C.

2. *L'Osservatore Romano*, English edition, Jan. 31, 1996.

11. Who completed and perfected God's Revelation?

Jesus Christ, the Eternal Word made flesh, by whom the fullness of Revelation comes to us.

12. How did Jesus confirm Revelation with divine guarantees?

Jesus confirmed Revelation by

- His words and deeds.
- The miracles he performed.
- His death and glorious Resurrection from the dead.
- The sending of the Holy Spirit, the Spirit of Truth, who leads and guides the Church in all truth about God and his plan for our salvation.

13. When did Jesus promise to send the Holy Spirit to guide the Church in all truth, and when was his promise fulfilled?

At the Last Supper, when Jesus said, "But when he comes, the Spirit of Truth, he will guide you in all truth" (*Jn* 16:13; cf. *Jn* 14:16). The Holy Spirit came on Pentecost (*Acts* 2).

14. What does the Church teach about *public* Revelation?

In Jesus Christ, God has revealed to us everything we need to know for our salvation. As stated in the *Catechism of the Catholic Church*: "Christ, the Son of God made man, is the Father's one, perfect, and unsurpassable Word. In him he has said everything; there will be no other word than this one" (*CCC* 65).

There will be no new public Revelation until the Second Coming of Jesus in glory. Jesus established the new and definitive Covenant that will never pass away. Therefore, public Revelation—that is, what God has revealed for our salvation through Christ as found in Sacred Tradition and Sacred Scripture, and which must be accepted in faith by all—ended with the death of the last Apostle.

15. What are *private* revelations?

Private revelations—for example, revelations given by God privately to saints, mystics, and others—even if approved by the Church, are not part of either Sacred Tradition or Scripture. They do not belong to the Deposit of Faith and do not bind in conscience. As the *Catechism* states, "It is not their role to improve or complete Christ's definitive Revelation, but to help live more fully by it in a certain period of history." (*CCC* 67).

Examples of private revelations that have been approved by the Church are apparitions of the Blessed Virgin Mary at Lourdes, France, and at Fatima, Portugal. These private revelations contain nothing that improves on or goes beyond the Revelation given to us already by Christ through the Church; they merely assist the faithful who follow them in living out their Christian vocation.

16. Can the Catholic faithful accept private revelations that claim to surpass or complete the Revelation of Jesus Christ?

No. As the *Catechism* goes on to say: "Christian faith cannot accept 'revelations' that claim to surpass or correct the Revelation of which Christ is the fulfillment, as is the case in certain non-Christian religions and also in certain recent sects which base themselves on such 'revelations'" (*CCC* 67).

Some examples of religions and recent sects that claim to possess revelations that surpass or correct the Revelation of Christ would be: Islam, the Latter-day Saints (Mormons), Jehovah's Witnesses, and Seventh Day Adventists. Both Muhammad, the founder of Islam, and Joseph Smith, the founder of Mormonism, claimed to have had private revelations from an angel. St. Paul warns against such claims when he says: "But even if we or an angel from heaven should preach to you a gospel other than the one that we preached to you, let that one be accursed" (*Gal* 1:8); and that "even Satan can masquerade as an angel of light" (*2 Cor* 11:14).

17. What is our *response* to God's Revelation of himself and his loving plan of salvation?

Obedience of faith: freely submitting our intellect and will to God's will as revealed to us by Jesus, and to the truth as revealed by him and the Holy Spirit (cf. *Jn* 14:16; 16:13) through the Catholic Church, "because its truth is guaranteed by God, who is Truth itself" (cf. *CCC* 144).

18. What is faith?

"Faith is the assurance of things hoped for, the conviction of things not seen" (*Heb* 11:1); "Faith is first of all a personal adherence of man to God. At the same time, and inseparably, it is a *free assent to the whole truth that God has revealed*" (*CCC* 150).

19. What assistance do we need to help us have faith in the revealed Word of God and to obey God's will as revealed therein?

The grace of God and the interior helps of the Holy Spirit: "Through [Jesus], we have received the grace . . . to bring about the obedience of faith" (*Rom* 1:5).

20. How do we obtain this grace and these interior helps of the Holy Spirit?

Through the sacraments; and through prayer, daily prayer, which is necessary in order to remain in God's grace and to be faithful and obedient to God's commands and his revealed truth.

21. Can God be known with certainty by the natural light of human reason?

Yes. God has created us in his own image and has endowed us with an intellect, or reasoning powers. By the natural light of human reason, we can attain certainty of knowledge of the existence of God from creation itself (cf. *CCC* 31, 36).

That the human mind is capable of knowing God with certainty from the created world is revealed by him in Scripture. As St. Paul says, "For what can be known about God is evident to them, because God made it evident to them. Ever since the creation of the world, his invisible attributes of eternal power and divinity have been able to be understood and perceived in what he has made" (*Rom* 1:19–20).

22. What do we call the ways of knowing that God exists by use of human reason?

They are called "proofs for the existence of God, not in the sense of proofs in the natural sciences, but rather in the sense of 'converging and convincing arguments,' which allow us to attain certainty about the truth" (*CCC* 31). The *Catechism* goes on to say that the ways of knowing God from creation are twofold: the physical world and the human person.

- First, from "The *world*: starting from movement, becoming, contingency, and the world's order and beauty, one can come to a knowledge of God as the origin and the end of the universe" (*CCC* 32). Our reason tells us that things in motion require a mover, and that there must have been a First Mover to set all things into motion. The First, or Unmoved, Mover is God. Our reason tells us that things do not come into existence and are not maintained in existence by themselves; it takes a Creator to create, to bring things into existence, and to keep things in existence; and that Creator is God. Further, all of creation is ordered; and our reason tells us that it takes an all-knowing mind and an all-powerful will to place all of creation in order and to keep all things in order (e.g., the planets in their orbits). That all-knowing and all-powerful Being is God.

- Second, from "The *human person*: With his openness to truth and beauty, his sense of moral goodness, his freedom and the voice of his conscience, with his longings for the infinite and for happiness, man questions himself about God's existence" (*CCC* 33).

23. **What do we call God revealing himself to us through creation by use of the natural light of human reason?**

Natural revelation.

24. **Through the use of our natural powers of reason, can we also come to a knowledge of basic religious and moral truths; e.g., the moral precepts contained in the Ten Commandments?**

Yes, there are "religious and moral truths which of themselves are not beyond the grasp of human reason" (Pius XII, *Humani generis*, 561: DS 3875; cf. *CCC* 38). St. Paul, speaking of the Gentiles who did not have the Law of Moses, says that "by nature [they] observe the prescriptions of the law [and] they show that the demands of the law are written in their hearts" (*Rom* 2:14–15). This ability we have to know basic right and wrong is referred to as "the natural law, written in our hearts by the Creator" (Pius XII, *Humani generis*, 561: DS 3875; cf. CCC 37).

25. **If the existence of God, as well as basic moral precepts, can be known through the use of human reason, why did God reveal himself to us through the Patriarchs and Prophets in the Old Testament, and fully through Jesus, his Son, in the New Testament?**

So that "those religious and moral truths which of themselves are not beyond the grasp of human reason, so that even in the present condition of the human race, they can be known by all men with ease, with firm certainty and with no admixture of error" (Pius XII, *Humani generis*, 561: *DS* 3876; cf. *Dei Filius* 2: *DS* 3005; *DV* 6; St. Thomas Aquinas, *S Th* I, 1,1; *CCC* 38).

26. **Is there another order of knowledge about God, which we cannot arrive at by use of our natural powers of reason? If so, what is this called?**

Yes. It is the order of divine, or supernatural, Revelation, through which God has revealed to us:

- Himself—the mystery of his own inner life as three divine Persons in One God (a truth beyond our powers of reason to attain).

- "[T]he mystery, his plan of loving goodness. . . . [which is] to communicate his own divine life to the men he freely created, in order to adopt them as his sons in his only-begotten Son" (*CCC* 50, 52). God has done this *by his direct intervention in the world*, in stages, beginning in the Old Testament, with Abraham, Moses, and the Prophets; and fully through Jesus Christ in the New Testament. (cf. *CCC* 53–67)

Chapter II

The Transmission
of Divine Revelation

27. How has the Revelation of Jesus Christ been handed on to us?

Through the Gospel, which is "the source of all saving truth and moral discipline." Jesus Christ commanded the Apostles to preach the Gospel (cf. *CCC* 75). It should be noted that the "Gospel" referred to here not only means the four Gospels of the New Testament; it means the *entire* saving message of Christ; the entire "Good News" of salvation that Christ has revealed.

28. How has the Gospel, the Revelation of Jesus Christ, been handed on to us?

In two ways:

- *Orally* by the Apostles through the spoken word of their preaching and teaching, by the example they gave, and by the institutions they established. The Apostles handed on faithfully "what they themselves had received—whether from the lips of Christ, from his way of life and his works, or whether they had learned it at the prompting of the Holy Spirit." (*DV* 7). This teaching has been handed down, and continues to be handed down, from the Apostles to their successors in office: the pope, and the bishops in union with the pope. (*see* Q.29, *infra.*)

- *In writing* "by those apostles and other men associated with the apostles who, under the inspiration of the same Holy Spirit, committed the message of salvation to writing" (*i.e.* the four Gospels and other New Testament books; *DV* 7).

29. **So there are two distinct modes of transmission of Divine Revelation, the Word of God as revealed fully by Jesus Christ. What are these two distinct modes called?**

Sacred Tradition and Sacred Scripture.

- *Sacred Tradition* is the revealed Word of God handed on or passed down *orally* (through preaching and teaching) by the Apostles to their successors in office: the pope, and the bishops in union with him. (Practically speaking, the oral preaching and teaching of Tradition are set down in writing; e.g., the papal bull defining the Immaculate Conception, as well as the very document under study here, *Dei Verbum*, are part of Sacred Tradition.) Art. 8 of *Dei Verbum* teaches that Sacred Tradition also encompasses all that the Church believes "in her doctrine, life and worship," which she "perpetuates and transmits to every generation"; and also includes the writings of the holy Fathers of the Church (the great saints from the first few centuries after Christ, known for their holiness of life, their fidelity to the Church, and the wisdom of their writings), who "are a witness to the life-giving presence of this Tradition" (*DV* 8).

- *Sacred Scripture*, which includes both the revealed Word of God *committed to writing* by the Apostles and apostolic men (the New Testament), and the writings of the Patriarchs and Prophets (the Old Testament), under the inspiration of the Holy Spirit.

Both Sacred Tradition and Sacred Scripture flow from the same divine Source (God); they are two distinct ways of expressing the same divinely revealed truth. (*see* Q.38, *infra*.)

30. **Is there proof from the Bible for what we call Sacred Tradition?**

Yes. St. Paul teaches, "Therefore, brothers, stand firm and hold fast to *the traditions* that you were taught, either by *oral statement* or by a letter of ours" (*2 Thess* 2:15); and the Apostle Jude teaches, " . . . and now I feel a need to write to encourage you to contend for the Faith that was once for all *handed down* [both orally and in writing] to the holy ones" (*Jude* 1:3; emphasis added in both passages).

31. What did the Apostles do to guarantee that the Gospel, the Good News of salvation, would be handed down to us in its entirety?

As the *Catechism* states: "In order that the full and living Gospel might always be preserved in the Church, the apostles left bishops as their successors. They gave them 'their own position of teaching authority' [so that] the apostolic preaching . . . [would] be preserved in a continuous line of succession until the end of time" (*DV* 7; St. Iraeneus, *Adv. haeres.* 3, 3, 1:PG 7, 848; Harvey 2,9; *DV* 8; cf. CCC 77).

32. But if we now have Sacred Scripture, why do we need Sacred Tradition? In other words, why did God arrange that there be successors to the Apostles, who were given the Apostles' own position of teaching authority, as pope and bishops?

To ensure that the apostolic preaching (Tradition) be handed on faithfully to all future generations, and that the Word of God committed to writing (Scripture) be interpreted faithfully and without error. This mission is carried on by the successors to the Apostles, who are guided in their work by the Holy Spirit—the same Holy Spirit who inspired the writing of the Scriptures (cf. CCC 77, 857, 861–862, 890).

33. How do we know that Peter and the Apostles and their successors in office (the pope and bishops) were given authority by Christ to teach, govern, and sanctify the Church?

Jesus founded his One, Holy, Catholic, and Apostolic Church on Peter and the Apostles and gave them and their successors in office full authority to teach, to govern, and to sanctify (cf. CCC 857, 890, 893–894; and *LG* 3: 18–25). The power of binding and loosing was given by Jesus first to Peter (*Mt* 16:19), and then to all the Apostles (*Mt* 18:18) with Peter as their head. But Jesus gave the keys of the kingdom of heaven to Peter alone (*Mt* 16:19); and Peter alone was commissioned by Jesus as head of the Apostles, with the words, "Feed my sheep" (*Jn* 21:15–17).

Jesus told his Apostles that they would teach in his name and with his authority: "He who hears you hears me; and he who despises you despises me" (*Lk* 10:16). At the Last

Supper, Jesus promised to send upon his Apostles and their successors in office the Holy Spirit, the Spirit of Truth, who "will be with you always" (*Jn* 14:16), and who "will guide you to all truth" (*Jn* 16:13). The Holy Spirit came on Pentecost.

34. What evidence is there to prove that popes and bishops succeeded Peter and the Apostles, and that they have authority to teach and govern in the Church?

Both Scripture and historical documents prove this. In *1 Tim* 3:1–13, St. Paul exhorts Timothy (himself a bishop) to select suitable men as bishops to govern the Church in Ephesus (cf. *Titus* 1:5–9). St. Clement of Rome, the fourth pope, wrote a famous letter in about A.D. 95, which shows that

- The Apostles appointed bishops to succeed themselves.

- Jesus willed that the Apostles appoint successors.

- All the faithful recognized the supreme authority of the Bishop of Rome (the pope). Pope St. Clement's letter was in response to a theological dispute in another geographical part of the Church, and those involved looked to him as the successor to Peter to settle the matter.

Another famous document is a work entitled *Adversus Haereses* ("Against Heretics") by St. Irenaeus, Bishop of Lyons from A.D. 177 to 200. It is cited in Footnote 3 of Par. 7 of *Dei Verbum*. St. Irenaeus, defending papal authority and papal succession from heretical attacks, wrote: "The faithful everywhere must needs agree with the Church at Rome; for in her the apostolic tradition had ever been preserved by the faithful from all parts of the world.

"The blessed Apostles, after they had founded and built the Church at Rome, handed over to Linus [the second pope] the office of Bishop. Paul mentions this Linus in his Epistles to Timothy [cf. *2 Tim* 4:21]. He was succeeded by Anacletus [the third pope], after whom Clement was appointed to the bishopric [of Rome], third in order from the Apostles. . . ." St. Irenaeus goes on to name all the successive popes up to the time when he was writing.

35. Why is the oral transmission of the Gospel called a "living" Tradition?

Because it continues to live on in the Church through the successors in office to the Apostles, who, by their preaching and teaching, carry on and define/interpret the teaching of Christ by means of the authority given to them with their office, under the guidance of the Holy Spirit (cf. *CCC* 78).

36. What does it mean to say that Sacred Tradition develops?

As Art. 8 of *Dei Verbum* states: "The Tradition that comes from the Apostles makes progress in the Church, with the help of the Holy Spirit. *There is a growth in insight into the realities and words that are being passed on.* This comes about in various ways . . . through the contemplation and study of believers . . . and from the preaching of those who have received, along with the right of their succession in the episcopate, the sure charism of truth. Thus, as the centuries go by, the Church is always advancing toward the plenitude of divine truth. . . ." (emphasis added).

The teaching explained above is commonly referred to as the "development of doctrine," which takes place under the guidance of the teaching office of the Church— i.e., the pope and the bishops united with him, who are in turn guided by the Holy Spirit, the Spirit of Truth.

Some examples of how doctrine develops within the Sacred Tradition of the Church, and how the Church "grows in insight into the realities and words that are passed on" from the Apostles to their successors, are the solemnly defined dogmas of papal infallibility (defined at Vatican Council I), of the Immaculate Conception of Mary (defined by Pope Pius IX in 1854), and of the Assumption of Our Lady, body and soul, into heaven (defined by Pope Pius XII in 1950). While the truths defined in these dogmas were *always* part of the Word of God revealed by Jesus Christ and handed on by the Apostles to their successors, the Church came to a deeper understanding of these truths down through the centuries under the guidance of the Holy Spirit.

Furthermore, in solemnly defining these dogmas, language was used which reflects this understanding on the part of the Church. For example, in his bull defining Mary's Immaculate Conception, *Ineffabilis Deus*, Pope Pius IX used the following words: "We declare, pronounce and define that the doctrine which holds that the Most Blessed Virgin Mary, at the first instant of her conception was preserved immune from all stain of sin, by a singular grace and privilege of the Omnipotent God, in view of the merits of Jesus Christ . . . was *revealed by God* and, therefore, must be firmly and constantly believed by all the faithful" (emphasis added).

37. What do we call the teaching authority, or teaching office, of the Church?

The *Magisterium*, from the Latin word *magister*, which means "teacher."

38. How are Sacred Tradition and Sacred Scripture related to each other?

Like two branches of a stream, they both flow "out from the same divine well-spring [God], come together in some fashion to form one thing, and move towards the same goal." *Both are the revealed Word of God under different forms* (cf. DV 9).

Sacred Tradition is the revealed Word of God given by Jesus to the Apostles, which has been and continues to be handed down orally through their successors, the pope and bishops in union with him, in their teaching and preaching, under the guidance of the Holy Spirit, whom Jesus promised his Apostles would "be with [them] always" (*Jn* 14:16), to "guide [them] to all truth" (*Jn* 16:13), and who came on Pentecost.

Sacred Scripture is the revealed Word of God put in writing under the inspiration of the Holy Spirit. The Word of God spoken by Jesus was put in writing in the Gospels, under the Holy Spirit's inspiration, in the years after Jesus ascended into heaven, as were the other books of the New Testament.

In a *broad sense*, Sacred Tradition includes all of Divine Revelation which comes down to us and encompasses, or takes within it, Sacred Scripture; for Scripture can be viewed as that part of Tradition (the oral preaching and teaching handed down from the Apostles) which was put into writing under the inspiration of the Holy Spirit.

The Second Vatican Council puts it this way in Art. 9 of *Dei Verbum*: "Sacred Scripture is the speech of God as it is put down in writing under the breath of the Holy Spirit. And Tradition transmits *in its entirety* the Word of God which has been entrusted to the Apostles by Christ the Lord and the Holy Spirit" (emphasis added).

It is important to realize that Sacred Tradition preceded (in time) the New Testament Scriptures, because the Apostles first handed down and taught orally what Jesus had taught them. Only later was this teaching committed to writing, under the inspiration of the Holy Spirit, in the Gospels. And of course the Letters of St. Paul and the other New Testament Letters, as well as the Book of Acts and the Book of Revelation were likewise inspired by the Holy Spirit. The *Catechism* makes this point when it teaches: "The first generation of Christians did not yet have a written New Testament, and the New Testament itself demonstrates the process of living Tradition" (*CCC* 83).

In a *narrower* sense, theologians use "Sacred Tradition" to mean, within this total Revelation handed on, that part of God's revealed Word that is not contained *explicitly* in Scripture (only *implicitly* there, in hidden form), but is *explicitly* taught in the Tradition, on matters of faith and morals (*see* Q. 42 & Q. 43, *infra*).

Furthermore, the *Catechism* distinguishes between Apostolic (Sacred) Tradition, and what are called "ecclesial" traditions: "Tradition is to be distinguished from the various theological, disciplinary, liturgical, or devotional traditions, born in the local churches [dioceses] over time. These are the particular forms, adapted to different places and times, in which the great Tradition is expressed. In the light of Tradition, these traditions can be retained, modified or even abandoned under the guidance of the Church's Magisterium" (*CCC* 83).

39. What is meant by the "Sacred Deposit" of the Word of God?

As Art. 10 of *Dei Verbum* states: "Sacred Tradition and Sacred Scripture make up *a single Sacred Deposit* of the Word of God, which is entrusted to the Church" (emphasis added). Christ "deposited" the Faith with his Apostles. And then, after his Ascension, he sent his Holy Spirit upon them at Pentecost to infallibly guide them and their successors in faithfully preserving and passing down the revealed Word of God

• In their preaching and teaching (Tradition).

• In what they committed to writing under the inspiration of the Holy Spirit (Scripture). As the *Catechism* teaches, "The apostles entrusted the 'Sacred deposit' of the faith (the *depositum fidei*)[3], contained in Sacred Scripture and Tradition, to the whole of the Church" (*CCC* 84).

40. Does the Church look to Scripture *alone* to teach the truth God has revealed?

No. Art. 9 of *Dei Verbum* teaches that "the Church does not draw her certainty about all revealed truths from the Holy Scriptures alone. Hence, both Scripture and Tradition must be accepted and honored with equal feelings of devotion and reverence."

41. So where is the divinely revealed Word of God to be found?

In both Sacred Tradition and Sacred Scripture.

42. Are all the truths we believe on matters of faith and morals found clearly and explicitly in Sacred Scripture?

No. For example, our belief that there are three divine Persons in One God is stated nowhere explicitly in Scripture. Neither does the Bible explicitly state that Jesus is one divine Person with two distinct natures, human and divine. These are both truths that were revealed by Christ; however, they were revealed only *implicitly* in the Scriptures. They were revealed *explicitly* through Sacred Tradition— by bishops in union with the pope at ecumenical councils in the early centuries of the Church.

Other examples are the defined Marian dogmas mentioned above, the doctrines of the Communion of the Saints and Purgatory, and the Church's teachings on the transmission of human life, which include the condemnation of abortion, contraception, sterilization, in vitro fertilization, etc.

---

3. Cf. *DV* 10.1; cf. *1 Tim* 6:20; *2 Tim* 1:12–14 (Vulg.)

**43. Who is the authoritative interpreter of the divinely re-
vealed Word of God, as it comes down to us through Sacred
Tradition and Sacred Scripture?**

The authoritative interpreter of the divinely revealed Word
of God is the official teaching authority (or teaching office)
of the Church, the Magisterium. As stated in Art. 10 of *Dei
Verbum*, "The task of giving an authentic interpretation of
the Word of God, whether in its written form [Scripture]
or in the form of Tradition, has been entrusted *to the living
teaching office of the Church alone. Its authority in this matter
is exercised in the name of Jesus Christ* . . . and with the help
of the Holy Spirit, it listens to [the Word of God] devotedly,
guards it with dedication, and expounds it faithfully" (emphasis added).

Thus Vatican II clearly teaches that in interpreting the divinely revealed Word of God, the pope and the bishops, when
they speak in union with him, exercise their authority *in
the name of Jesus Christ.* When the pope himself speaks definitively on matters of faith or morals, or when the pope
with the bishops does so (for example, at an ecumenical
council), it is Christ himself speaking (cf. *CCC* 85).

**44. Why is the Magisterium the authoritative interpreter of
Sacred Scripture?**

The Magisterium is the authoritative interpreter of Sacred
Scripture because the same Holy Spirit who inspired the
writing of Scripture infallibly guides the Magisterium in correctly and truthfully interpreting Scripture. This means that
*no one individual or large group of individuals, including theo-
logians, can authoritatively interpret Sacred Scripture.* We must
always look to the Church's Magisterium for sure guidance
and the final say in such matters, for only it has "authority exercised in the name of Christ."

Art. 8 of *Dei Verbum* declares: "By means of the same Tradition the full canon of the sacred books is known to the
Church and the Holy Scriptures themselves are more thor-
oughly understood and constantly actualized in the Church.
Thus God, who spoke in the past, continues to converse with
the spouse of his beloved Son [i.e., the Church]. And the
Holy Spirit, through whom the living voice of the Gospel

rings out in the Church—and through her in the world—
leads believers to the full truth. . . ."

Also, it must be remembered that the Holy Spirit guided the
teaching authority of the Church in determining which books
and letters (of the many that were circulating in the first
few centuries of the Church) were truly inspired by God
and should be included in the Bible (*see* Q's 55–57, *infra*).
As St. Augustine (quoted in *CCC* 119) once said, "But I would
not believe in the Gospel, had not the authority of the Catholic Church already moved me."

**45. Why is the Magisterium the authoritative interpreter of
Sacred *Tradition*?**

The Magisterium is the authoritative interpreter of Sacred
Tradition because only the pope and the bishops united with
him have the sure guidance of the Holy Spirit to authoritatively interpret the revealed Word of God as passed down
through Tradition. Moreover, in their teaching they form
and further define the Tradition itself.

The Holy Spirit continues to infallibly guide the Church by
the revealed Word of God throughout the ages in the areas of faith and morals; and the Church applies this revealed
Word, deposited with the Apostles, to new situations or technologies that arise. This is precisely why it is called a *living* Tradition. The following concrete examples will help to
illuminate this concept:

- At the beginning of his 1991 encyclical, *Centesimus annus*
  ("On the Hundredth Anniversary of Rerum novarum")
  Pope John Paul II, in setting forth the basis for the Church's
  social teaching, condemned socialism and communism and
  their atheistic view of the human person (Art. 13), and
  also the consumerism of affluent nations, which "totally
  reduces man to the sphere of economics and the satisfac-
  tion of material needs" (Art. 19). The Pontiff wrote that
  "the Church's Tradition, which, being ever living and vital,
  builds upon . . . what the Apostles passed down to the
  Church in the name of Jesus Christ. . . . The Church's Tradition . . . contains 'what is old'—received and passed
  down from the very beginning—and which enables us
  [himself as pope and popes before him] to interpret the

'new things' in the midst of which the life of the Church and the world unfolds" (Art. 3).

- In May 1995 Pope John Paul II issued an apostolic letter, "On Reserving Priestly Ordination to Men Alone," in which he said, "I declare that the Church has no authority whatsoever to confer priestly ordination on women and that this judgment is to be definitively held by all the Church's faithful." Several months later, in response to questions raised on the nature of this papal teaching, the Sacred Congregation for the Doctrine of the Faith issued a clarifying statement on the pope's letter, saying that this teaching "is founded on the written word of God and from the beginning constantly preserved and applied in the Tradition of the Church"; and that "the Roman Pontiff . . . handed on this same teaching by a formal declaration . . . as belonging to the Deposit of the Faith."

- In teaching that there is *an inseparable connection between the unitive/love meaning and the procreative/life meaning of the conjugal act,* and thereby condemning contraception and sterilization (which unnaturally and artificially separate the love of the marital embrace from the procreation of human life) as well as such technologies as in vitro fertilization and cloning (which unnaturally separate human life from the loving marital embrace), Pope Paul VI, in his 1968 encyclical *Humanae vitae* ("On the Transmission of Human Life"), said this was "a teaching founded upon the natural law, *illuminated and enriched by Divine Revelation*" (Art. 4; emphasis added).

- In his 1995 encyclical, *Evangelium vitae* ("The Gospel of Life"), Pope John Paul II, in addressing the issue of the direct taking of innocent human life, especially at its beginning (through abortion and infanticide) and at its end (through euthanasia, or mercy killing), stated: "[B]y the authority which Christ conferred upon Peter and his Successors, and in communion with the Bishops of the Catholic Church, *I confirm that the direct and voluntary killing of an innocent human being is always gravely immoral.* This doctrine, based upon that unwritten law which man, in the light of reason, finds in his own heart (cf. *Rom* 2:14–15), is reaffirmed by Sacred Scripture, transmitted by the Tradition of the Church and taught by the ordinary and universal Magisterium" (Art. 57; emphasis in original).

- As is evident from the quotations above from both *Humanae Vitae* and *Evangelium Vitae*, the Magisterium uses the divinely revealed Word of God, deposited by Christ with the Apostles and passed down through their successors, to shed light upon the natural law that is written in the heart of man and known through the light of human reason. See *Lumen Gentium* 3: 25; and *CCC* 891–892 for a fuller explanation of the means by which the Magisterium arrives at definitive teachings on:

  — Matters of faith or morals (whether by "extraordinary" or "ordinary" means).

  — Infallible definitions that must be adhered to with the *obedience of faith.*

  — Other teachings by "ordinary" means, which must be adhered to with *religious assent.*

46. How are Sacred Tradition, Sacred Scripture, and the Magisterium all related?

"[I]n the supremely wise arrangement of God," says Art. 10 of *Dei Verbum*, "Sacred Tradition, Sacred Scripture, and the Magisterium of the Church are so connected and associated that one of them cannot stand without the others. Working together, each in its own way under the action of the one Holy Spirit, they all contribute effectively to the salvation of souls."

The chart below shows that Sacred Scripture cannot be viewed in a vacuum, apart or in isolation from Sacred Tradition and the Magisterium:

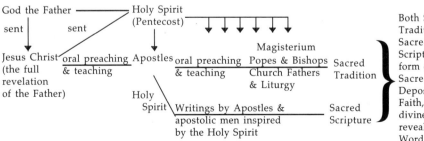

The Pope, and bishops united with him, under the guidance of the Holy Spirit authoritatively interpret Sacred Scripture, and interpret and define Sacred Tradition.

It was indeed "supremely wise" for Jesus, in founding his Church, to constitute it with a visible hierarchy, and to give supreme teaching authority to Peter and the Apostles, and to their successors in office, under the guidance of the Holy Spirit, the Spirit of Truth. Jesus wanted to guarantee that his teachings—his revealed Word in both Tradition and Scripture, would be handed on faithfully and without error, and not be distorted. (cf. CCC 857, 889–890).

Only through the Magisterium, under the guidance of the Holy Spirit, has the teaching that Christ committed to his Apostles been preserved in its entirety throughout the ages; and the fundamental error of every heresy has been to break with the official teaching authority of the Church, as represented and put forth by the Vicar of Christ on earth, the pope. But as Art. 10 of *Dei Verbum* points out: "Yet this Magisterium is not superior to the Word of God, but is its servant. It teaches only what has been handed on to it." (cf. CCC 86).

47. What happens when there is no recognized authority to interpret Scripture?

Many different interpretations result, some of which are erroneous and lead to separations from Christ's Mystical Body, the Church. The central error of non-Catholics in their approach to the Bible is their belief that there exists no authoritative and infallible interpreter of Scripture. This belief also rejects the idea of a visible hierarchy in the Church with a supreme authority in the person of the pope. And it rejects the whole notion of Sacred Tradition. This approach was expressed in Martin Luther's term, *sola Scriptura*—by "Scripture alone." But the Bible itself refutes the idea that individuals alone and apart from the Church can always interpret the Bible correctly. St. Peter himself warns us, "In them [the letters of St. Paul] there are some things hard to understand that the ignorant and unstable *distort to their own destruction*, just as they do the other scriptures" (2 Pet 3:16; emphasis added).

Interestingly, it was the letters of St. Paul that Martin Luther (who was a Catholic priest and Augustinian monk) misinterpreted and distorted in arriving at his teaching that "faith alone" without good works suffices for salvation. By rejecting the idea of a supreme authority in the Church which faithfully interprets Scripture and by embracing a "Scripture alone" approach, Martin Luther was able to posit his own way to salvation ("faith alone, apart from good works"), which was in opposition to 1,500 years of Church teaching as found in Sacred Tradition. St. Peter's words were truly prophetic in regard to Martin Luther, and to every religious leader and sect that sets itself apart from the Catholic Church and claims authority to interpret the Bible in a manner inconsistent with Tradition.

It was for a very practical reason that Jesus intended Peter and the Apostles, and their successors in office, to have supreme teaching authority in his Church: that no one would be led astray, and that there would be no division within his Church. At the Last Supper, Jesus prayed that "all may be one" (*Jn* 17:21).

Chapter III

Sacred Scripture:
Its Divine Inspiration
and Interpretation

48. Who is the principal, or chief, author of Sacred Scripture?

God the Holy Spirit (cf. *CCC* 105).

49. Why does the Church teach that God the Holy Spirit is the principal author of Scripture?

Because the books of the Old and New Testaments, "whole and entire, with all their parts" were "written under the inspiration of the Holy Spirit" and "have God as their Author" (*DV* 11).

50. What does it mean to say that the books of the Bible were written "under the inspiration of the Holy Spirit"?

It means that "[t]o compose the sacred books, God chose certain men who . . . made full use of their own faculties and powers so that, *though he acted in them and by them, it was as true authors that they consigned to writing whatever he wanted written, and no more*" (emphasis added; *DV* 11).

51. What does the term "canon" mean?

"Rule," or "standard."

52. What is meant by the "sacred canon" of the Holy Bible?

The official, or standard, list of books in the Bible.

53. How many books make up the canon of the Bible in the Old Testament and in the New Testament?

In all 72 books: 45 in the Old Testament and 27 in the New Testament. But if the Book of Lamentations is counted as a separate book—as is sometimes done, rather than being included in the Book of Jeremiah—then the number of Old Testament books is 46, and the total number of books in the Bible is 73 (cf. *CCC* 120).

54. Why does the Church teach that all 45 books of the Old Testament and all 27 books of the New Testament are sacred and canonical; that is, belong to the canon?

Because they were all written, in their entirety, in all their parts, "under the inspiration of the Holy Spirit" and "have God as their author." (*DV* 11).

55. Who has the authority to determine which books are inspired by God; that is, which books constitute the canon of the Holy Bible?

The Catholic Church, because it alone is guided infallibly by the Holy Spirit, the Spirit of Truth. The same Holy Spirit who inspired the writing of the Scriptures guided the Catholic Church in determining which books were truly inspired, and therefore properly parts of the canon. As the *Catechism of the Catholic Church* states, "It was by the apostolic Tradition that the Church discerned which writings are to be included in the list of sacred books" (*CCC* 120).

56. When did the Catholic Church first determine that all 45 books of the Old Testament and all 27 books of the New Testament are sacred and canonical; that is, that these books are the inspired Word of God?

By the end of the fourth century, all 72 books of the Holy Bible were accepted by the Church as constituting the official canon of Sacred Scripture.

In the first few centuries after Christ, numerous writings in circulation were said to have being inspired by God. Some were written before Christ (e.g., the "Book of Henoch"), and some written after Christ bore the names of the Apostles (e.g., the "Gospel of Peter" and the "Gospel of Philip") and were alleged to have been written by them. These are known as *apocrypha*, which means "hidden": they were supposedly hidden for generations, until they were finally discovered. The Catholic Church, under the guidance of the Holy Spirit, infallibly pronounced which books of both the Old and New Testaments were truly written under the inspiration of the Holy Spirit and authored by the Apostles and other holy men. The Church made these pronouncements at the Council of Hippo in 393, and the Council of Carthage in 397. The Council of Trent in 1546 reaffirmed the declaration of both of these earlier councils concerning the canon of Sacred Scripture.

57. **Do non-Catholics (for example, Protestants) hold that all 72 books of the Bible are inspired by God and part of the canon? Why or why not?**

No. Protestants say that some books are not part of the canon. For example, one-time Catholic priest and Augustinian monk Martin Luther excluded *1 & 2 Maccabees* from the canon because *2 Maccabees* 12:46 speaks of "making atonement for the dead that they might be freed from sin." This reveals a place of purgation after death (called Purgatory). Since Luther rejected Purgatory, he therefore excluded these books from the canon of the Bible.

Other Protestant "reformers" followed suit. Luther also threw out the Book of James, because *Jas* 2:17 reveals that "faith of itself, if it does not have works, is dead;" and Luther, followed by other Protestants, held that "faith alone" saves us.

In order to conform the Bible to their own brand of theology, Luther and others held that these and other books of the Bible—books that the Catholic Church for over 1,000 years had held to be canonical and inspired by God—were "apocrypha." In so doing, they rejected the revealed Word of God. As pointed out earlier, to do this necessitated rejecting the whole notion of Sacred Tradition, and the supreme authority that oversees and guides Tradition—the authority of Peter's successor, the pope. This is the reason why Protestant Bibles have fewer books than the true Bible, which is the Catholic Bible.

58. **Can there be any errors in the writing/composition of the Bible?**

No, there can be no errors, because to admit the possibility of error in the writing of any part of the Bible would be to deny divine inspiration. The Holy Spirit is the Spirit of Truth, and as the principal author of Scripture, he could not have erred; nor could he have inspired the human authors to err in writing what they wrote. As *Dei Verbum*, Art. 11 states, the Holy Spirit "acted in [the human authors] and by them" so that they wrote "whatever he [God] wanted written, and no more."

"Since therefore all that the inspired authors or sacred writers affirm should be regarded as affirmed by the Holy Spirit, we must acknowledge that the books of Scripture firmly, faithfully, and *without error*, teach that truth which God, for the sake of our salvation, wished to see confided to the Sacred Scriptures" (emphasis added).

59. Is there any proof for this position in Scripture?

Yes. In *2 Tim* 3:16, St. Paul teaches that "*All* Scripture is *inspired by God* and is useful for teaching, for refutation, for correction . . ." (emphasis added). And St. Peter writes that "we possess the prophetic message that is altogether reliable. . . . Know this first of all, that there is no prophecy of Scripture that is a matter of personal interpretation, for no prophecy ever came through human will; but rather human beings moved by the Holy Spirit spoke under the influence of God" (*2 Pet* 1:19–21).

60. Art. 11 of *Dei Verbum* states: "[T]he books of Scripture firmly, faithfully, and without error, teach that truth which God, for the sake of our salvation, wished to see confided to the Sacred Scriptures." Does this mean, as some claim, that the Bible is free from error *only* in regard to "truths concerning our salvation"—that is, on matters of faith and morals, but not in everything else; and that therefore there can be some errors in the Bible?

No. Immediately following the sentence quoted above in Art. 11 of *Dei Verbum* is a footnote (no. 5); and cited in Footnote 5 are a number of Church documents, among which is a famous letter by St. Augustine to St. Jerome, in which the former states that as to the books of Scripture, he "believes most firmly" that "none of their writers has fallen into error."

Also cited in Footnote 5 is Pope Leo XIII's 1893 encyclical, *Providentissimus Deus* ("On the Study of Sacred Scripture"). In this encyclical, Pope Leo XIII declares: "It is absolutely wrong and forbidden either to narrow inspiration to certain parts only of Holy Scripture or to admit that the sacred writer has erred. As to the system of those who . . . do not hesitate to concede that divine inspiration regards the things of faith and morals, and nothing beyond . . . this system cannot be tolerated."

Pope Leo XIII goes on to say that "All the books which the Church receives as sacred and canonical are written wholly and entirely, with all their parts, at the dictation of the Holy Spirit; and so far is it from being possible that any error can coexist with inspiration, that inspiration not only is essentially incompatible with error, but excludes and rejects it as absolutely and necessarily as it is impossible that God himself, the supreme Truth, can utter that which is not true. This is the ancient and unchanging faith of the Church, solemnly defined in the Councils of Florence and of Trent, and finally confirmed and more expressly formulated by the [First] Council of the Vatican."

Earlier in this encyclical, Leo XIII excoriates those "who with great labor carry out and publish investigations . . . whose chief purpose . . . is too often to find mistakes in the sacred writings and so shake and weaken their authority."

"It is true, no doubt," he says, "that copyists [i.e., those who copied the Scriptures hundreds of years ago] have made mistakes in the text of the Bible; this question, when it arises, should be carefully considered on its merits, and the fact not too easily admitted, but only in those passages where the proof is clear."

In the above passages it is plain that Pope Leo XIII allows for the possibility of human error in *copying* the Scriptures; but excludes the possibility of error on the part of the Holy Spirit in inspiring the sacred writer in any part of Scripture.

Footnote 5 of *Dei Verbum*, Art. 11, also cites Pope Pius XII's 1943 encyclical, *Divino Afflante Spiritu* ("On the Promotion of Biblical Studies"). At the very beginning of this encyclical, the Holy Father soundly rejects the theory—adhered to by many 20th century biblical "critics"—that divine inspiration and freedom from error extend only to matters of faith and morals. He writes: "When subsequently some Catholic writers . . . ventured to restrict the truth of Sacred Scripture solely to matters of faith and morals, and to regard other matters, whether in the domain of physical science or history, as . . . in no wise connected with faith, Our Predecessor of immortal memory, Leo XIII, in the Encyclical Letter *Providentissimus Deus* . . . rightly condemned these errors. . . .". Pius XII calls for implementation of the art of "textual criticism"; that is, correcting ancient copies of Scripture and purifying them "from the corruptions due to the carelessness of the [ancient] copyists," so as to "be freed from glosses and omissions, from the interchange and repetition of words and from all other kinds of mistakes, which are wont to make their way gradually into writings handed down through many centuries".

As St. Paul states: "*All* Scripture is inspired by God and is useful for teaching, for refutation, for correction. . ." (*2 Tim* 3:16–17; emphasis added). And the *Catechism*, citing Art. 11 of *Dei Verbum* , teaches: "God is the author of Sacred Scripture because he inspired its human authors; he acts in them and by means of them. He thus gives assurance that their writings teach without error his saving truth (*CCC* 136; cf. *DV* 11)". Thus the Bible itself testifies to the truth that there are no errors in Scripture, because it is *all, in its entirety,* inspired by God; and Sacred Tradition, in the form of Church councils and papal encyclicals, confirms this revealed truth.

61. Are all things found in the Bible to be interpreted as literally and factually true?

Art. 11 of *Dei Verbum* teaches that "all that the inspired authors or sacred writers affirm should be regarded as affirmed by the Holy Spirit." This means that all that the sacred writers affirm, or assert, *as true* should be regarded as affirmed and asserted as true by the Holy Spirit. Therefore, only those things in Scripture that were *intended to be taken as true* by the human author (and the Holy Spirit) must be regarded as factually true; as literal assertions of fact. Alternatively, if the sacred author (and the Holy Spirit) did *not* intend something to be taken as factually true, it should not be held as true, but rather should be interpreted in another way.

As the *Catechism* states on this point: "To interpret Scripture correctly, the reader must be attentive to what the human authors truly wanted to affirm and to what God wanted to reveal to us by their words" (CCC 109). In No. 110 the *Catechism* continues: "In order to discover *the sacred authors' intention*, the reader must take into account the conditions of their time and culture, the literary genres in use at that time, and the modes of feeling, speaking, and narrating then current." (emphasis in original). It then quotes *Dei Verbum*, Art. 12: "For the fact is that truth is differently presented and expressed in the various types of historical writing, in prophetical and poetical texts, and in other forms of literary expression."

Hence the task of the biblical scholar/interpreter is to study the ancient cultures, modes of expression, etc., and to try to determine whether the statement or story was intended by the sacred author (and the Holy Spirit) to be understood as literally and factually true, or whether it was intended to be understood in an allegorical or poetical sense—that is, to convey a religious or moral truth, but not necessarily to be taken as an absolutely literal fact.

For example, while the Church teaches that the human race did in fact descend from Adam and Eve (based on the Genesis account of the creation of man), it does not teach that the Genesis account of God creating the world in six "days" must be interpreted as six 24-hour periods. The sacred writer may have intended the word "day" to be understood in a poetical sense, to mean a period of time, possibly billions of years—for "with the Lord, one day is like a thousand years. . . ." (2 *Pet* 3:8). The basic truths the sacred writer intended to affirm were that God created all from nothing over a period of time, and created Adam and Eve as the progenitors of the human race.

Similarly, the Book of Genesis makes frequent use of anthropomorphisms—the attribution of human qualities to God—which are used for poetic effect but are not to be taken literally. For example, we read that God "rested on the seventh day from all the work he had undertaken" (*Gen* 2:2) (when in reality, God is always active in maintaining all of creation in existence); that Adam and Eve "heard the sound of God moving about in the garden" (*Gen* 3:8); and that "the Lord came down to see the city and the tower [of Babel] that the men had built" (*Gen* 11:5).

In the encyclical *Divino Afflante Spiritu*, Pope Pius XII teaches that looking to the intention of the sacred writer is a way to help resolve some of the difficulties scholars encounter in trying to interpret certain biblical texts, and to provide an alternative for saying that Scripture contains "errors":

"Hence the Catholic commentator . . . in explaining the Sacred Scripture and in demonstrating and proving its immunity from all error, should also . . . determine . . . to what extent the manner of expression or the literary mode adopted by the sacred writer may lead to a correct and genuine interpretation. . . . Not infrequently . . . when some persons reproachfully charge the sacred writers with some historical error or inaccuracy in the recording of facts, on closer examination it turns out to be *nothing else than those customary modes of expression and narration peculiar to the ancients. . . .*" (Art. 38; emphasis added). The pope also wisely adds: "No wonder if to one or other question no solution wholly satisfactory will ever be found, since sometimes we have to do with matters *obscure in themselves and too remote from our times and our experience. . . .*" (Art. 45; emphasis added).

62. What guidelines must be used in interpreting Sacred Scripture?

Quoting Art. 12 of *Dei Verbum*, the *Catechism* says that we must always read and interpret Sacred Scripture "in the light of the same Spirit by whom it was written," that is with its divine authorship in mind (Nos. 111-114). This means that:

- Attention must be devoted *"to the content and unity of the whole of Scripture,"* which "is a unity by reason of the unity of God's plan."

- Scripture must be read within *"the living Tradition of the whole Church,"* for "it is the Holy Spirit who gives her [the Church] the spiritual interpretation of the Scripture."

- One must *"be attentive to the analogy of faith."* Reading Scripture in light of the "analogy of faith" means that every statement must be interpreted in light of the entire body of revealed truths, in conformity with all the doctrines the Church teaches in both Sacred Tradition and Sacred Scripture. One cannot interpret a passage in a way that conflicts with either a doctrine of the Faith or accepted interpretations of other passages.

63. What are the different "senses" of Scripture?

Paragraph 115 of the *Catechism* declares: "According to an ancient tradition, one can distinguish between two *senses* of Scripture: the *literal* and the *spiritual*, the latter being subdivided into the *allegorical*, *moral*, and *anagogical* senses."

* "The *literal sense* is the meaning conveyed by the words of Scripture. . . . 'All other senses of Sacred Scripture are based on the literal'" (*CCC* 116; St. Thomas Aquinas, *S. Th.* I, 1, 10 ad 1). The precise meaning of the "literal" sense was elaborated more fully in a 1993 document entitled *The Interpretation of the Bible in the Church*,[4] published by the Pontifical Biblical Commission (which Commission, says Joseph Cardinal Ratzinger in the Preface, after Vatican II "is not an organ of the teaching office [Magisterium], but . . . they enjoy the confidence of the teaching office"). As explained in this document: "The literal sense is not to be confused with the 'literalist' sense to which fundamentalists are attached. . . . One must understand the text according to the literary conventions of the time. When a text is metaphorical, its literal sense is not that which flows immediately from a word-to-word translation (e.g., 'Let your loins be girt': *Lk* 12:35), but that which corresponds to the metaphorical use of these terms ('Be ready for action'). . . . The literal sense of Scripture is that which has been expressed directly by the inspired human authors. Since it is the fruit of inspiration, this sense is also intended by God, as the principal author. One arrives at this sense by means of a careful analysis of the text, within its literary and historical context."[5]

* "The *spiritual sense* . . . [means that] the realities and events about which [a passage] speaks can be signs:
  — "The *allegorical sense* . . . [by which events acquire] significance in Christ; thus the crossing of the Red Sea is a sign or type of Christ's victory and also of Christian Baptism (cf. *1 Cor* 10:2).
  — "The *moral sense*. The events reported in Scripture ought to lead us to act justly (cf. *1 Cor* 10:11; cf. *Heb* 3:7–4:11).

---

4. See *Origins, CNS Documentary Service,* Jan. 6, 1994 (Vol. 23, No. 29), pp. 498ff.
5. *Ibid.,* p. 512.

— "The *anagogical sense* (Greek: *anagoge*, 'leading'). We can view realities and events in terms of their eternal significance . . . thus the Church on earth is a sign of the heavenly Jerusalem" (CCC 117; cf. *Rev* 21:1–22:5).

The 1993 Pontifical Biblical Commission document explains: "As a general rule *we can define the spiritual sense . . . as the meaning expressed by the biblical texts when read*, under the influence of the Holy Spirit, *in the context of the paschal mystery of Christ* [his death and resurrection] and the new life which flows from it. . . . In it the New Testament recognizes the fulfillment of the [Old Testament] Scriptures" (emphasis added). It also states that the paschal event of Jesus "sheds fresh light upon the ancient texts and causes them to undergo a change in meaning. In particular, certain texts which in ancient times had to be thought of as hyperbole (e.g., the oracle where God, speaking of a son of David, promised to establish his throne 'forever' in *2 Sam* 7:12–13), must now be taken literally, because 'Christ, having been raised from the dead, dies no more' (*Rom* 6:9)."[6]

The document goes on to point out: "When a biblical text relates directly to the paschal mystery of Christ or to the new life which results from it, its literal sense is already a spiritual sense. Such is regularly the case in the New Testament. It follows that it is most often in dealing with the Old Testament that Christian exegesis speaks of the spiritual sense. . . . While there is a distinction between the two senses, the spiritual sense can never be stripped of its connection with the literal sense."[7]

64. Who is it that ultimately determines the manner, or sense, in which the Scriptures are interpreted?

As stated in Art. 12 of *Dei Verbum*, "the manner of interpreting Scripture is ultimately subject to the judgment of the Church which exercises the divinely conferred commission and ministry of watching over and interpreting the Word of God."

---

6. *Ibid.*

7. *Ibid.*

Chapter IV
The Old Testament

65. To what people in the Old Testament did God reveal himself and his loving plan of salvation for the whole human race?

To the Jewish people, beginning with Abraham, and later through Moses and the Prophets.

66. What is meant by the "economy" of salvation?

The "economy" of salvation means essentially everything that is contained within God's loving plan of salvation as it unfolded.

67. What was the central purpose of God's plan of salvation as it unfolded in the Old Testament?

The central purpose was to prepare for the coming of the Savior, Jesus Christ, who would establish the New and Eternal Covenant by shedding his own blood for our sins, and thereby usher in the messianic kingdom.

68. Is God's plan revealed clearly and explicitly in the Old Testament?

No. As stated in Art. 15 of *Dei Verbum*, in the Old Testament "the mystery of our salvation is present in a hidden way."

69. How does the Old Testament relate to the New Testament, and the New to the Old?

"God, the inspirer and author of both Testaments, in his wisdom has so brought it about that the New should be hidden in the Old and that the Old should be made manifest in the New" (*DV* 16).

Chapter V
The New Testament

70. What is the purpose of the writings in the New Testament?

To "hand on the ultimate truth of God's Revelation," in the Person of Jesus Christ (CCC 124).

71. What is the central object of the New Testament writings?

It is Jesus Christ, the Eternal Word Made Flesh, who "established on earth the kingdom of God, revealed his Father and himself by his deeds and words; and by his death, resurrection and glorious ascension, as well as by sending the Holy Spirit, completed his work" (*DV* 17).

72. Why do the Gospels hold a special place among all the inspired writings of Scripture?

Because the Gospels "are our principal source for the life and teaching of the Incarnate Word, our Savior." (*DV* 18)

73. What does the Council mean by saying that "the Church has always and everywhere maintained, and continues to maintain, the apostolic origin of the four Gospels"?

Dei Verbum, Art. 18, says: "*The Apostles . . . and others of the apostolic age* handed on to us in writing the same message they had preached, the foundation of our Faith: the fourfold Gospel, according to Matthew, Mark, Luke and John" (emphasis added). Therefore, to say that the four Gospels are of "apostolic origin" means that they were written, under the inspiration of the Holy Spirit, either by the Apostles themselves, or by "others of the apostolic age." The Apostles who wrote the Gospels were St. Matthew and St. John; "others of the apostolic age" refers to St. Mark and St. Luke.

74. How do we know that the four Gospels faithfully hand on what Jesus really did and taught?

We know this because, as the Church authoritatively teaches in Art. 19 of *Dei Verbum:* "Holy Mother Church has firmly and with absolute constancy maintained and continues to maintain, that the four Gospels, . . . whose historicity she unhesitatingly affirms, *faithfully hand on what Jesus, the Son of God, while He lived among men, really did and taught for their eternal salvation*, until the day he was taken up (cf. *Acts* 1:1–2). For, after the ascension of the Lord, the apostles handed on to their hearers what He had said and done, but with that fuller understanding which they, instructed by the glorious events of Christ and enlightened by the Spirit of truth, now enjoyed" (emphasis added).

75. Is there any proof for this teaching in the Bible?

Yes. In the beginning of his Gospel, St. Luke writes: "Since many have undertaken to compile a narrative of the events that have been fulfilled among us, just as *those who were eyewitnesses and ministers of the Word have handed them down to us*, I too have decided . . . to write it down in an orderly sequence for you, most excellent Theophilus, *so that you may realize the certainty of the teachings you have received*" (*Lk* 1:1–4) (emphasis added). In *Acts* 1:1–2 [cited in Art. 19], St. Luke writes once again to Theophilus: "In the first book, Theophilus, I dealt with all that Jesus did and taught until the day he was taken up, after giving instructions through the Holy Spirit to the Apostles whom he had chosen."

Furthermore, the footnotes (2 and 3) to the section of Art. 19 of *Dei Verbum* quoted above contain citations to numerous passages from the Gospel of St. John in support of this teaching. Two citations are taken from Jesus' words to his Apostles at the Last Supper: "The Advocate, the Holy Spirit the Father will send in my name—he will teach you everything and *remind you of all that I told you*" (*Jn* 14:26) and "But when he comes, the Spirit of Truth, he will *guide you in all truth*" (*Jn* 16:13) (emphasis added in both quotes).

76. The Gospels sometimes contain different versions of Jesus' teachings. Does not this fact raise a problem to the position that the Gospels "faithfully hand on what Jesus . . . really did and taught"?

No. The apparent "problem" is resolved by the teaching in Art. 19 of *Dei Verbum*, which proclaims, "The sacred authors, in writing the four Gospels, selected certain of the many elements which had been handed on, either orally or already in written form, others they synthesized or explained with an eye to the situation of the churches [i.e., dioceses], [all] the while sustaining the form of preaching, *but always in such a fashion that they have told us the honest truth about Jesus.* Whether they relied on their own memory and recollections or on the testimony of those who 'from the beginning were eyewitnesses and ministers of the Word,' *their purpose in writing was that we might know 'the truth' concerning the things of which we have been informed"* (cf. *Lk* 1:2–4; emphasis added).

The Church here teaches, first of all, that in writing their respective Gospels the Evangelists used both *oral* and *written* sources. The Apostles SS. Matthew and John relied principally on the *oral preaching and deeds* of Jesus to which they were eyewitnesses. SS. Mark and Luke used what was handed down to them orally by those who "from the beginning were eyewitnesses and ministers to the Word"—that is, the Apostles, who in handing on the teaching of Jesus to SS. Mark and Luke, now enjoyed (as Art. 19 of *Dei Verbum* teaches) "that fuller understanding" of Jesus' words and deeds, after having been "enlightened by the Spirit of Truth."

In writing their Gospels the Evangelists also made use of other eyewitnesses as well, such as the Blessed Virgin Mary (*see* discussion by Pope John Paul II regarding Mary as a source for the birth and infancy narratives of Jesus in Q. 80, *infra*). Additionally, Art. 19 of *Dei Verbum* teaches that the Evangelists made use of what was "already in written form"; that is, what was already in writing but in unfinished (Gospel) form. Here we see reference to the various stages in the writing of the Gospels: the life and teaching of Jesus; the oral preaching by the Apostles; and the actual writing of the Gospels (cf. *CCC* 126).

Secondly, in the above quote from Art. 19 of *Dei Verbum* the Church teaches that the four Evangelists selected certain events and sayings of Jesus ("selected certain of the many elements which had been handed on"), because they were writing "with an eye to the situation of the churches;" that is, with a view toward the varying situations, needs, and religious and cultural backgrounds of the people in the "local churches"—the areas within the universal Church that are now called dioceses.

Thirdly, while the precise words of Jesus as recorded in the four Gospels may vary slightly, they nonetheless contain the true substance of his teaching. As Art. 19 of *Dei Verbum* states, while the Evangelists may have selected certain things or synthesized others with a view to the audience for which they were writing, all the while they "sustain the form of [Christ's] preaching, always in such a fashion that they have told us the honest truth about Jesus."

A footnote (no. 4) immediately follows the above-quoted sentence and cites an official Church document, an Instruction entitled *Sancta Mater Ecclesia* ("Holy Mother Church"). This Instruction, dealing with the historical truth of the Gospels, was prepared by the Pontifical Biblical Commission in 1964, and was formally approved by Pope Paul VI on April 21, 1964, before *Dei Verbum* was completed (Nov. 18, 1965). The Instruction clarifies the sentence in Art. 19 of *Dei Verbum* which precedes Footnote 4, for the Instruction states in part: "The truth of the [Gospel] narrative is not affected in the slightest by the fact that the Evangelists report the sayings or the doings of our Lord in a different order, and that they use different words to express what he said, not keeping to the very letter, but nevertheless preserving the sense."

77. Why did Pope Paul VI and the Pontifical Biblical Commission deem it necessary to defend the historical truth of the words and deeds of Jesus found in the Gospels?

Because, as *Sancta Mater Ecclesia* declares: "Today . . . in many publications, circulated far and wide, the truth of the events and sayings recorded in the Gospels is being challenged." And the Instruction also gives some reasons why various biblical "experts" were challenging the truth of the events and sayings recorded in the Gospels.

The promoters of these theories, says *Sancta Mater Ecclesia*, "led astray by rationalistic prejudices, refuse to admit that there is a supernatural order, or that a personal God intervenes in the world by revelation properly so called, or that miracles and prophesies are possible and have actually occurred. There are others who have as their starting point a wrong notion of faith, taking it that faith is indifferent to historical truth, and is indeed incompatible with it. Others practically deny *a priori* the historical value and character of the documents of Revelation. Others finally there are who on the one hand underestimate the authority which the Apostles had as witnesses of Christ. . . , whilst on the other hand they overestimate the creative power of the [primitive Christian] community. *All these aberrations are not only opposed to Catholic doctrine, but are also devoid of any scientific foundation, and are foreign to the genuine principles of the historical method"* (emphasis added).

Sancta Mater Ecclesia further says that biblical scholars may make use of what is called the "historical-critical method"— a method of looking at texts of Scripture "critically" from the standpoint of historical development—but "must be circumspect in doing so, however, because the method is often found alloyed with principles of a philosophical or theological nature which are quite inadmissible."

In the *Commentary on the Documents of Vatican II,*[8] the historical notes on *Dei Verbum* point out that the draft version of Art. 19 of *Dei Verbum*, originally submitted to the Second Vatican Council Fathers for approval, included the words, "proceeding from the creative power of the early Christian community," after the words, "they [the sacred authors] have told us the honest truth about Jesus." These additional words, says commentator Beda Rigaux, "clearly referred to the ideas of R. Bultmann [an early 20th century professor of Scripture]," and "in the course of the revisions [of the draft of *Dei Verbum*] of 1964, at the request of a number of highly qualified fathers [bishops], the Commission [of bishops] dropped" these additional words from the text.

In his Erasmus Lecture in New York on Jan. 27, 1988, called *Foundations and Approaches of Biblical Exegesis,*[9] Joseph Cardinal Ratzinger, Prefect of the Sacred Congregation for the Doctrine of the Faith, echoed the words and teaching of *Sancta Mater Ecclesia.* Cardinal Ratzinger said that the problem with much of modern "scientific" Scripture study, in its use (or misuse) of the "historical-critical method," is a

---

8. Gen. ed., Herbert Vorgrimler, et al., Vol. III, Ch. 5, "The New Testament," by Beda Rigaux (New York: Herder and Herder, 1967), p. 258.

9. *Origins,* Feb. 11, 1988 (Vol. 17, No. 35), pp. 594 ff.

philosophical one: scholars like Rudolf Bultmann and others early in this century applied *"a model of evolution* . . . to
the analysis of biblical texts;" therefore, he said, "the non-
historicity [untruthfulness] of the miracle stories was no
question anymore. The only thing one needed to do yet was
to explain how these miracle stories came about"—that is,
were "invented"—in the early Christian communities.

The real philosophic presupposition for the "evolutionary/
non-historical" view of biblical texts, said Ratzinger, lies in
the philosophy of Immanuel Kant, which leads to a denial
of supernatural intervention by God in human history. "In
theological terms," he said, "this means that . . . what might
otherwise seem like a direct proclamation of the divine can
only be myth, whose *laws of development* [evolution] can be
discovered. *It is with this basic conviction that Bultmann, with
the majority of modern exegetes, read the Bible."* Thus, said
Ratzinger, "At its core, the debate about modern exegesis
is not a dispute among historians: it is rather a philosophical dispute."[10]

In the Preface to the 1993 Pontifical Biblical Commission
document, Cardinal Ratzinger noted that with the rise of
the historical-critical method, "new possibilities for understanding the biblical word opened up . . . though, just as
with all human endeavors, this method contained hidden
dangers along with its positive possibilities." One danger,
said the cardinal, is that modern biblical methods can become so bound up in "the search for the original" that "the
genuine author, God, is removed" from consideration."[11] The
Pontifical Commission itself said that while many Catholic
scholars continue to make wide use of the historical-critical method, "many members of the faithful . . . judge the
method deficient from the point of view of faith . . . They
insist that the result of scientific exegesis is only to provoke
perplexity and doubt upon numerous points . . . [and] to
adopt positions contrary to the faith of the Church on matters
of great importance, such as the virginal conception of Jesus
and his miracles, and even his resurrection and divinity."[12]

---

10. *Ibid.*, p. 599 (emphases added).

11. *Origins*, Jan. 6, 1994, *op. cit.*, p. 499.

12. *Ibid.*, p. 500.

The Pontifical Biblical Commission went on to make the following admission: "We must frankly accept that certain hermeneutical [interpretative] theories are inadequate for interpreting Scripture. For example, Bultmann's existentialist interpretation tends to enclose the Christian message within the constraints of a particular philosophy. Moreover, by virtue of the presuppositions insisted upon in this hermeneutic, the religious message of the Bible is for the most part emptied of its objective reality (by means of excessive 'demythologization'). . . . Philosophy becomes the norm of interpretation, rather than an instrument for understanding the central object of all interpretation: the person of Jesus Christ and the saving events accomplished in human history."[13]

78. **Practically speaking, what means have been used by some modern-day biblical scholars to challenge and/or deny the historical truth of the words and actions of Jesus?**

They have posited a theory that separates the historical event of Jesus' life from the writing of the Gospel accounts. In so doing, they deny the apostolic origin of the Gospels; i.e., that the Gospels were written by the Evangelists whose names they bear—by those who were either eyewitnesses to the words and actions of Jesus (St. Matthew and St. John), or those who spoke with eyewitnesses (St. Mark and St. Luke).

Instead, by use of the historical-critical method, a theory of "evolutionary development" is substituted, holding that the four Gospels were written not by "the Apostles . . . and others of the apostolic age" (as Art. 18 of *Dei Verbum* teaches), but rather were written by unknown authors some 40–70 years after Jesus' Death and Resurrection,[14] and were the result of the early Christian community reflecting on what Jesus meant to them in their current situation. By denying the apostolic origin of the Gospels and the testimony of eyewitnesses to the words and actions of Jesus, it then becomes very easy to challenge, and even to deny, the historical truth of the events recorded in the Gospels.

---

13. *Ibid.*, p. 511

14. It is commonly held by most orthodox biblical scholars that the Apostle John authored his Gospel about the year 96 (*see* Q. 83, *infra.*).

79. Do many modern-day biblical scholars hold to the theory of non-apostolic authorship of the Gospels?

That such theories are widely held among many present-day biblical commentators is clear from the words of Fr. Raymond Brown, probably the most widely read Catholic biblical scholar, who himself holds to these modern theories. In his book, *Responses to 101 Questions on the Bible*,[15] Father Brown says: "The view that the evangelists were not themselves eyewitnesses of the public ministry of Jesus would be held in about 95% of contemporary critical scholarship." He goes on to say that "the designations that you find in your New Testament, such as 'The Gospel According to Matthew' . . . are the results of late-second-century scholarship attempting to identify the authors of works that had no identification."[16]

80. What are some examples of this "evolutionary" view of the writing of the Gospels, which lead to the words and actions of Jesus being challenged and/or denied, and even to positions contrary to the Faith?

One example is found in *The New Testament: An Introduction*,[17] a book that has been used in Scripture classes at Catholic colleges and theology schools. In their work, authors Norman Perrin (former professor at the University of Chicago) and Dennis Duling (of Canisius College) state that "earliest Christianity *created* a Jesus tradition—a tradition of sayings of Jesus and stories about him—based partly on actual reminiscence of his ministry and teaching, partly on experience of him in their present, and partly on an expectation of him in the future . . . earliest Christianity also treated Jesus as the Hellenistic world in general treated its heroic figures: it *developed legends* increasingly depicting him as a man of miraculous knowledge and power. There are legendary stories in the gospels, such as the Stilling of the Storm and the Walking on the Water. . . ."[18]

---

15. (New York: Paulist Press, 1990).

16. *Ibid.*, pp. 59-60.

17. (New York: Harcourt Brace Javonovich, Publishers, 1982).

18. *Ibid.*, p. 398 (emphasis added).

Perrin and Duling go on to tell the reader: "The New Testament writers present us with material *put on the lips of the Jesus of the Gospels by the church. But this is not the historical Jesus* and the material attributed to him in fact had a long and complex history of transmission in the tradition of the church before it reached the form in which we find it. . . . It had constantly been edited and interpreted in response to the changing needs and insights of the communities of Christians through which it passed."[19] The authors then cite the writings of Rudolf Bultmann, and say that in his works, "*The narratives about Jesus, like the biographical framework of the total story of Jesus itself, were judged to have little historical value.*"[20]

Fr. Raymond Brown, in his book *101 Questions*, applies a theory of "evolutionary development" to the writing of the Gospels in general, and in particular to the infancy narratives (of the conception and birth of Jesus) in the Gospels of SS. Matthew and Luke. In so doing, he concludes that "there are reasons for thinking that the birth stories [of Jesus], which are found in the first two chapters of Matthew and the first two chapters of Luke, are not historical in some, or even many details."[21] In his earlier book, *The Birth of the Messiah: A Commentary on the Infancy Narratives in Matthew and Luke,*[22] Father Brown explains why he can hold such a position: he all but dismisses what is traditionally held to be the basis for the stories of the conception and birth of Jesus in the Gospels—the eyewitness testimony from the Blessed Virgin Mary related to St. Luke. Father Brown says that this view is "not impossible but faces formidable difficulties."[23]

Father Brown's theory challenging the historical truth of the infancy narratives has implications in matters concerning dogma and faith. He claims that "The historical-critical method of interpretation does not offer adequate evidence to resolve the historicity of either the virginal conception or the perpetual virginity of Mary," but he says: "I [Brown]

---

19. *Ibid.*, pp.400–401 (emphasis added).

20. *Ibid.*, p. 402 (emphasis added).

21. *Op. cit.*, p. 76.

22. (Garden City, New York: Doubleday & Co., Inc., 1977).

23. *Ibid.*, p. 526.

believe Mary remained a virgin because the Roman Catholic Church teaches this doctrine."[24]

In his Wednesday audience address of Jan. 28, 1987,[25] Pope John Paul II refuted the theories of Father Brown outlined above. The Holy Father declared: "The events linked to the conception and birth of Jesus are contained in the first chapters of Matthew and Luke, generally called 'the infancy Gospels.'" And the Pontiff noted that "To identify *the source of the infancy narrative* one must go back to St. Luke's remark: '*Mary kept all these things,* pondering them in her heart' (*Lk* 2:19). Luke states this twice. . . . The evangelist himself provides us with the elements to identify in the Mother of Jesus one of the sources of the information used by him in writing 'the infancy Gospel.' Mary, who 'kept these things in her heart,' could bear witness, after Christ's death and resurrection, in regard to what concerned herself and her role as Mother, *precisely in the apostolic period when the New Testament texts were being written. . . .*" (emphasis added in last sentence). John Paul II then stated:: "Mary was a *virgin* before the birth of Jesus, and she remained a virgin in giving birth and after the birth. *That is the truth presented by the New Testament texts,* and which was expressed both by the Fifth Ecumenical Council at Constantinople in 553, which speaks of Mary as *ever virgin,* and also by the Lateran Council in 649. . . ." (emphasis added in second instance).

Finally, the problem with Father Brown's position—that "the historical-critical method does not offer adequate evidence" to support the virginal conception or perpetual virginity of Mary but he believes it "because the Catholic Church teaches this doctrine"—is that the Church *bases* its teaching on Mary's virginity on the historical truth of the Gospel narratives. As John Paul II pointed out in the same 1987 audience: "The text of Luke's Gospel is the *basis* of the Church's teaching on the motherhood and virginity of Mary. . . ." (emphasis added). To challenge or deny the historical truth of the Gospel on this point (as well as many others) is to undermine the faith.

---

24. "Exegesis and Dogma: A Review of Two Marian Studies,"Rev. John McHugh, with a reply by Rev. Raymond Brown, S.S., *Ampleforth Review* 85 (1980), p. 43.

25. *L'Osservatore Romano,* English edition, Feb. 2, 1987.

Fr. John Meier, a professor of New Testament studies at Catholic University of America, is even bolder in challenging the perpetual virginity of Mary based on "historical-critical" grounds. In his 1991 presidential address to the The Catholic Biblical Association (he was president of the association at the time) at Loyola Marymount University, he said that on "historical" grounds, "the most probable opinion is that the brothers and sisters of Jesus were true siblings."[26] In an interview that appeared in the December 1997 issue of *St. Anthony Messenger*, Father Meier, in answer to the question "Can historians address the Resurrection [of Jesus]?" said: "We can verify as historians that Jesus existed and that certain events reported in the Gospels happened in history, yet historians can never prove the Resurrection in the same way . . . the Resurrection stands outside of the sort of questing by way of historical, critical research. . . ."[27]

Compare Father Meier's "critical" approach, which can lead to doubt and confusion, with the teaching of the *Catechism*, which looks to the eyewitness testimony of the Apostles as recorded in the Gospels for historical proof of the Resurrection: "By means of touch and the sharing of a meal, the risen Jesus establishes direct contact with his disciples. He invites them in this way to recognize that he is not a ghost *and above all to verify that the risen body in which he appears to them is the same body that had been tortured and crucified*, for it still bears the traces of his passion" (CCC 645; cf. *Lk* 24:30,39–40,41–43; *Jn* 20:20,27;21:9,13–15; emphasis added).

In No. 647 the *Catechism* teaches: "Although the Resurrection was a historical event *that could be verified* by the sign of the empty tomb and by the reality of the apostles' encounters with the risen Christ, still it remains at the very heart of the mystery of faith as something that transcends and surpasses history" (emphasis added).

Still another example of the historical-critical method gone awry is something called the "Jesus Seminar." Since 1985, a group of biblical professors and commentators, both non-Catholic and Catholic, have gathered yearly at a meeting

---

26. *Des Moines Sunday Register*, Dec. 24, 1995, p. 3A.
27. p. 37.

under this name. As reported in *U.S. News & World Report* (April 8, 1996), this group examines "the historicity of words and deeds of Jesus from the Gospels" and then reports the results "in press releases and in books. . . ." The group (which includes Fr. John Meier) "concluded that no more than 20 percent of the sayings and even fewer of the deeds attributed to Jesus are authentic. Among the castoffs: the Lord's Prayer, the sayings from the cross and any claims of Jesus to divinity, the virgin birth, most of his miracles and his bodily resurrection."[28]

A co-chairman of the Seminar is John Dominic Crossan, an ex-priest who is now married and a professor at DePaul University in Chicago. According to the *U.S. News* article, Crossan "rejects most of the Gospel record as inaccurate. . . . Biblical accounts of the Last Supper and appearances of the risen Jesus, he says, are merely attempts by his devout followers to express their 'continued experience' of his presence after the Crucifixion."[29] According to a *Time* magazine article (April 10, 1995) that reported on the Jesus Seminar the year before, Crossan argues that "since the Crucifixion was conducted by Roman soldiers, Jesus' body was most likely left on the Cross or tossed into a shallow grave to be eaten by scavenger dogs, crows or other wild beasts."[30]

81. What do the statements quoted in the previous question demonstrate?

They demonstrate that when the Church's official teaching is disregarded as to the historical truth of the Gospels, the "historical-critical method" can be misused and lead not only to a denial of Jesus' words and deeds, but also to a rejection of the most basic truths of the Faith, and even to outright blasphemy: that the body of Jesus was "eaten by scavenger dogs. . . ."

82. Can Catholics legitimately hold to the "evolutionary" theory of the writing of the Gospels: that they were written not by the Evangelists whose names they bear, but rather

28. p. 49.

29. p. 52.

30. p. 70

are the products of "the creative power of the early Christian community," and were written late in the first century by unknown authors?

No, Catholics cannot hold to this position, which is contrary to the constant teaching of the Church. As Art. 18 of *Dei Verbum* clearly teaches, "The Church has always and everywhere maintained, and continues to maintain, the apostolic origin of the four Gospels. *The Apostles preached . . . and then, under the inspiration of the Holy Spirit, they and others of the apostolic age handed on to us in writing the same message they had preached, the foundation of our faith: the fourfold Gospel, according to Matthew, Mark, Luke and John*" (emphasis added). And Art. 19 of *Dei Verbum* directly refutes the view that the Evangelists were not themselves eyewitnesses of the public ministry of Jesus or did not talk with eyewitnesses: "The sacred authors, in writing the four Gospels . . . relied on their own memory and recollections or on the testimony of those who 'from the beginning were eyewitnesses of the Word. . . .'"

The teaching expressed in Arts. 18 and 19 of *Dei Verbum* dates back to the last century, when the papal Magisterium first responded to such evolutionary theories. In his 1893 encyclical letter, *Providentissimus Deus* ("On the Study of Sacred Scripture") Pope Leo XIII teaches (as the 1964 Instruction on the *Historical Truth of the Gospels* would later teach, and Cardinal Ratzinger himself would later emphasize) that the foundation for such theories is rooted in philosophical error: "The Rationalists . . . deny that there is any such thing as revelation or inspiration . . . the prophecies and the oracles of God are to them either predictions made up *after* the event or forecasts formed by the light of nature; the miracles and the wonders of God's power are not what they are said to be, but the startling effects of natural law, or else tricks and myths; and *the apostolic Gospels and writings are not the work of the Apostles at all*" (emphasis added). Pope Leo XIII referred to these positions as "detestable errors" which "are obtruded on the world as the peremptory pronouncements of a certain newly invented 'free science'. . . ."

The 1964 Instruction calls the position of those who "underestimate the authority which the Apostles had as witnesses of Christ [in the Gospels] . . . and overestimate the creative capacity of the community itself . . . aberrations . . .

not only opposed to Catholic doctrine, but also devoid of any scientific foundation, and . . . foreign to the genuine principles of the historical method." Recall, for our purposes here, that the 1964 Instruction is cited in Footnote 4 of Art. 19 of *Dei Verbum*.

83. **Is there any early historical evidence to support the Church's teaching that the Gospels were written by "the Apostles and other apostolic men"? And can we estimate when the Gospels were written?**

Yes to both questions.

- **The Gospel of St. Matthew**

    Authorship

    We have early testimony from the Fathers of the Church that St. Matthew wrote the Gospel that bears his name: Eusebius, in his *Ecclesiastical History* (III, 39, 16), quotes Papias, Bishop of Hierapolis in Phrygia (Asia Minor)—who had been a disciple of St. John the Evangelist—as saying, "Matthew wrote the Oracles of the Lord in the Hebrew language." (Note: The language of the Hebrews in Palestine at the time of Jesus was Aramaic.)

    At the end of the second century St. Irenaeus, who also was familiar with the writings of Papias, wrote: "Matthew published his Gospel among the Hebrews in their own tongue" (*Adversus Haereses*, III, 1,1). Significantly, Footnote 1 to Art. 18 of *Dei Verbum* (which follows the sentence, "The Apostles . . . and others of the apostolic age handed on to us in writing . . . the fourfold Gospel according to Matthew, Mark, Luke, and John.") cites St. Irenaeus' work, *Adversus Haereses*.

    Dating

    Traditional Catholic teaching, based on written testimonies going back to the beginning of the second century, holds that St. Matthew was the first to write his Gospel. The original Aramaic version disappeared after the destruction of Jerusalem in A.D. 70. Immediately afterward a Greek edition appeared, which version the Church accepted as canonical. The *Replies* of the Pontifical Biblical Commission (June 19, 1911) stated that the original text of St. Matthew's Gospel is to be dated prior to the destruction of Jerusalem in A.D. 70, and even prior to St. Paul's journey to Rome in the year 60. Today many scholars estimate the date to be about the year 50.[31]

• The Gospel of St. Mark

Authorship

Early writings unanimously support St. Mark as the author of the Gospel that bears his name, and as the disciple and interpreter of the Apostle St. Peter. Once again, Eusebius quotes Papias, a disciple of St. John (who writing in about the year 125) said: "Mark, having been the interpreter of Peter, wrote accurately, though not in order, all that he remembered of the things said or done by the Lord. For he [Mark] had neither heard the Lord nor been his follower, but afterwards, as I said, he was the follower of Peter. . . ." (*Eccles. Hist.*, III, 39, 15).

St. Irenaeus, who was a disciple of St. Polycarp (who himself was a disciple of St. John the Evangelist), writes that, "After the departure of Peter and Paul, Mark, Peter's disciple and interpreter, delivered to us in writing what Peter had preached" (*Adv. Haer.*, III, 1,1 and 10,6). On June 26, 1914, the Pontifical Biblical Commission issued a *Reply* expressly teaching that St. Mark is the author of the Gospel that bears his name. These are just two of the many testimonies verifying St. Mark as the author of the Gospel that bears his name.

Dating

On July 26, 1912, the same Pontifical Biblical Commission issued a *Reply* stating that the Gospel of St. Mark must be dated earlier than the year 70—this based upon Ch. 13 of his Gospel, which recounts Jesus' words about the future destruction of the Temple in Jerusalem, which the Commission said must be understood as a true prophecy, written

---

31. Cf. *A Guide to the Bible*, Antonio Fuentes, Dublin: Four Courts Press, 1993, p. 175; and *The Navarre Bible: Saint Matthew's Gospel*, Dublin: Four Courts Press, 1988, Introduction, p. 17. But for other theories regarding the possible original languages and dates of composition of the Gospels of Matthew, Mark, and Luke, see Msgr. Michael Wrenn's article, *The Language and Dating of the Gospels*, Position Papers, December 1997, Dublin.

before the event. Scholars offer two possible dates of authorship: either about the year 60, or between 64 and 67.[32]

- ## The Gospel of St. Luke

Authorship

Catholic Tradition is unanimous in attributing the authorship of the third Gospel to St. Luke, who was a friend and companion of St. Paul (cf. *Col* 4:14; *2 Tim* 4:11; *Philem* 24). Most significant is a list of New Testament books known as the "Muratorian Canon." This list, which was organized by an unknown author in the late second century, contains notes made on each book.

Its notes on St. Luke's Gospel say: "The third book of the Gospel is that according to Luke. This Luke, a physician . . . wrote down what he had heard, for . . . he had not known the Lord in the flesh, and having obtained such information as he could he began his account with the birth of John."

About the year 400, St. Jerome wrote in his book, *On Famous Men*: "Luke, a physician from Antioch . . . a follower of St. Paul, who accompanied him on his journeys, wrote a Gospel. . . ." Other witnesses to this Tradition include Origen, Clement of Alexandria, Tertullian, St. Irenaeus, and Eusebius.

The Pontifical Biblical Commission on June 26, 1912, stated: 'The clear verdict of Tradition—showing extraordinary unanimity from the beginnings of the Church and confirmed by manifold evidence, namely the explicit attestations of the holy Fathers and ecclesiastical writers, the quotations and allusions occurring in their writings . . . and also internal reasons drawn from the text of the sacred books—impose the definite affirmation that Mark, the disciple and interpreter of Peter, and Luke, the doctor, the assistant and companion of Paul, really were the authors of the Gospels that are attributed to them respectively.'

Dating

A *Reply* of the Pontifical Biblical Commission of June 26, 1912, states that St. Luke's Gospel was written prior to

---

32. Cf. Fuentes, *op. cit.*, pp. 177–78; *The Navarre Bible: St. Mark*, Dublin: Four Courts Press, 1985, Introduction, pp. 59-60.

the fall of Jerusalem (A.D. 70). The Commission further specified that because in the *Acts of the Apostles* (1:1) St. Luke makes mention of his "first book", his Gospel must have been written before Acts. Further, because the Acts of the Apostles ends with a description of St. Paul's ministry near the end of his first imprisonment in Rome (which was in A.D. 63), St. Luke's Gospel must be dated near the end of the year 62 or the beginning of the year 63.[33]

• The Gospel of St. John

Authorship

Ancient tradition is very strong in ascribing the writing of the fourth Gospel to St. John. The Muratorian Canon contains a prologue against the heretic Marcion, which says that "the Gospel of John was communicated and proclaimed to the churches by John himself, while he was still alive, according to Papias of Hierapolis." Papias was a disciple of St. John.

St. Irenaeus writes: "John, the disciple of the Lord, who had even rested on his breast, himself published a Gospel, while he was living in Ephesus" (*Adv. Haer.*, III, 1,1). Other early witnesses include Tertullian, Origen, and Clement of Alexandria. According to Clement of Alexandria, "John, perceiving that the other Evangelists had set forth the human side of the Person of Jesus, at the instance of his disciples composed a spiritual Gospel" (cited by Eusebius, *Eccles. Hist.*, VI, 14).

Dating

The church historian Eusebius tells us that Clement of Alexandria passed on a tradition that St. John wrote his Gospel after the other three Evangelists wrote theirs (*Ecclesiastical History*, VI, 14, 5–7). Most scholars date St. John's writing of the Gospel around the year A.D. 96.[34]

---

33. Cf. Fuentes, *op. cit.*, p. 181; and *The Navarre Bible: St. Luke* (Dublin: Four Courts Press, 1987, Introduction. pp. 15-16, 18.

34. Cf. *The Navarre Bible: St. John*, Dublin: Four Courts Press, 1987, Introduction, pp. 23-24.

84. **Why is it important to hold to the teaching of *Dei Verbum* that the Gospels are of "apostolic origin"; that is, the true authorship of the Gospels is by SS. Matthew, Mark, Luke, and John?**

Because, as the foregoing questions and answers (77–80) indicate, *to deny that the authors of the Gospels were themselves eyewitnesses, or that they relied on testimony of "those who from the beginning were eyewitnesses" to the words and deeds of Jesus Christ, is to open the door to calling into question the historical truth of the Gospels.* And that truth is that the Gospels "faithfully hand on what Jesus, the Son of God, while he lived among men, really did and taught for their eternal salvation" (*DV* 19; cf. *Acts* 1: 1-2).

85. **Has the historical-critical method and a "model of evolution" (referred to by Cardinal Ratzinger) been used in analyzing biblical texts other than the four Gospels?**

Yes. This approach has also been used in analyzing the Pentateuch; that is, the first five books of the Bible: Genesis, Exodus, Leviticus, Numbers, and Deuteronomy. Although neither *Dei Verbum* nor the *Catechism of the Catholic Church* deals with the authorship of these (or other) Old Testament books, it has been the subject of much controversy in biblical circles for more than a century.

Traditionally, Moses was recognized as the inspired author of the Pentateuch. Beginning in the last century, what is now known as the *documentary theory* of authorship became popular. This theory maintains that three different, independent sources (Yahwist, Elohist, and Priestly Codex) from three different time periods (all hundreds of years after Moses lived) were responsible for writing parts of the first four books, and a fourth source for writing Deuteronomy. Under this theory, when strictly applied, Moses is not considered to have authored the Pentateuch.

This theory was rejected by the Pontifical Biblical Commission in its decree of June 27, 1906, which upheld Mosaic authorship based on "the cumulative evidence of many passages of both Testaments [Old and New], the unbroken unanimity of the Jewish people, and furthermore the constant tradition of the Church besides the internal indications furnished by the text itself." But in its decree the Commission did not rule out the possibility that in the centuries after the death of Moses, additions might have been made to parts of the Pentateuch by an inspired author, who also might have updated forms of the language.

Although many, if not most, biblical scholars today reject Mosaic authorship, the tide seems to be turning back toward recognizing Moses as having been the "substantial" author of most of the Pentateuch (recognizing that others may have actually written it —secretaries, amanuenses, et al.). Fr. William Most, in his book, *Free From All Error*,[35] cites a computer study done at the Technion Institute in Israel, in which "twenty thousand words of Genesis, in Hebrew, were fed into a computer programmed to make a thorough linguistic analysis of words, phrases, and passages in the text. The project coordinator, Yehuda Radday, reached a controversial conclusion: 'It is most probable that the Book of Genesis was written by one person' (*Newsweek*, Sept. 28, 1981, p. 59)."[36]

And in their book, *Before Abraham Was: A Provocative Challenge to the Documentary Hypothesis*,[37] Drs. Isaac Kikawada and Arthur Quinn present a very persuasive case for the single authorship of the first eleven chapters of Genesis, thereby refuting the strongest basis for the documentary hypothesis (which claims multiple authorship, over the course of centuries, for *Gen* 1–11).

86. **What is the purpose of the Epistles, or Letters, of St. Paul and the other apostolic writings in the New Testament?**

"In accordance with the wise design of God these [other] writings . . . formulate more and more precisely [Christ's] authentic teaching, preach the saving power of Christ's divine work and foretell its glorious consummation" (*DV* 20).

---

35. Rev. William G. Most, *Free From All Error: Authorship, Inerrancy, Historicity of Scripture, Church Teaching, and Modern Scripture Scholars* (Libertyville, Illinois: Franciscan Marytown Press, 1985).

36. *Ibid.*, p. 18.

37. (San Francisco: Ignatius Press, reprinted in 1989).

Chapter VI

Sacred Scripture in the Life of the Church

87. What is the purpose of Sacred Scripture in the life of the Church today?

The Church regards "the Scriptures, taken together with Sacred Tradition, as the supreme rule of her Faith." The Scriptures "can serve the Church as her support and vigor and the children of the Church as strength for their faith, food for the soul, and a pure and lasting font of spiritual life" (*DV* 21).

88. Does the Church promote the use and reading of the Bible among the faithful?

Yes. "Access to Sacred Scripture ought to be wide open to the Christian faithful" (*DV* 22).

89. How does the Church provide the faithful with ready access to the Bible?

By seeing that "suitable and correct translations are made into various languages, especially from the original texts of the sacred books." (*DV* 22)

90. What does the Church encourage in moving toward "a more profound understanding of the Sacred Scriptures"?

The Church "duly fosters the study of the Fathers, both Eastern and Western, and of the sacred liturgies." (*DV* 23)

91. Who are the Fathers of the Church?

They are writers in the early Church who have been given the title Father in light of four characteristics:

- *Antiquity.* They lived in the early centuries of Christendom.
- *Orthodoxy.* Their writings were faithful to the teaching of the Church on matters of faith and morals.

- *Sanctity.* Each of them lived a holy life.

- *Approbation.* Their writings have been approved by the Church, either formally by a pope or ecumenical council referring to them as Fathers, or informally by the Church recognizing their writings as next to Sacred Scripture in authority and forming a part of Sacred Tradition. (cf. *DV* 8, which states that "the Holy Fathers are a witness to the life-giving presence of this Tradition.")

92. What is meant by the terms "Eastern" and "Western" Fathers?

The Fathers are commonly divided into the Eastern (Greek) and the Western (Latin), depending on which language their works were written in. Some of the Eastern/Greek Fathers are St. Athanasius, St. Basil, and St. John Chrysostom. And St. Irenaeus, St. Jerome, and St. Augustine are among the Western Fathers. It is generally agreed that the last of the Western Fathers was St. Isidore of Seville (560?–636), and the last Eastern Father was St. John Damascene (675–749).

93. Why are the writings of the Fathers of the Church so important to the study of Sacred Scripture?

The Fathers are important because their writings have helped to form part of Sacred Tradition, and to provide authoritative interpretations of Sacred Scripture. According to the solemnly defined teaching of Vatican Council I: "In matters of faith and morals affecting the structure of Christian doctrine, that sense of Sacred Scripture is to be considered as true which holy Mother Church has held and now holds . . . therefore, no one is allowed to interpret Sacred Scripture contrary to this sense nor contrary to the unanimous agreement of the Fathers."[38]

Pope Leo XIII, in his 1893 encyclical letter, *Providentissimus Deus* ("On the Study of Sacred Scripture"), teaches that "it is permitted to no one to interpret Holy Scripture against . . . the unanimous agreement of the Fathers" and that "the Holy Fathers are of supreme authority, whenever they interpret in one and the same manner any text of the Bible,

---

38. Vatican I, *Dogmatic Constitution on the Catholic Faith*, Ch. 2: *DS* 1788 (3007).

as pertaining to the doctrine of faith and morals; for their unanimity clearly evinces that such interpretation has come down from the Apostles as a matter of Catholic Faith."

This same pope goes on to say that "the opinion of the Fathers is also of very great weight when they treat of these matters in their capacity as Doctors unofficially . . . because they are men of eminent sanctity and of ardent zeal for the truth, on whom God has bestowed a more ample measure of his light. Wherefore the expositor should make it his duty to follow their footsteps with all reverence, and to use their labors with intelligent appreciation."

Pope Pius XII, in his 1943 encyclical letter, *Divino Afflante Spiritu* ("On the Promotion of Biblical Studies"), teaches that those who study Sacred Scripture should try to discover the two senses, or meanings, of the text: the "literal" sense (that is, the general meaning) and the "spiritual" sense, that is, the deeper, spiritual meaning of the text that God intends but that may not be readily apparent to the reader. Pope Leo XIII also notes that Catholics will find "invaluable help in an assiduous study of those works, in which the Holy Fathers, the Doctors of the Church and the renowned interpreters of past ages have explained the Sacred Books. For . . . by reason of the office assigned to them by God in the Church, they are distinguished by a certain subtle insight into heavenly things and by a marvelous keenness of intellect, which enables them to penetrate the very innermost meaning of the divine word and bring to light all that can help to elucidate the teaching of Christ and promote holiness of life" (par. 28).

In commenting on the value of the Fathers' contributions to the study and interpretation of Scripture, the 1993 Pontifical Biblical Commission document (*The Interpretation of the Bible in the Church*) had this to say: "The Fathers of the Church, who had a particular role in the process of the formation of the canon, likewise have a foundational role in the relation to the living tradition which unceasingly accompanies and guides the Church's reading and interpretation of Scripture. Within the broader current of the great tradition, the particular contribution of patristic exegesis consists in this: to have drawn out from the totality of Scripture the basic orientations which shaped the doctrinal tradition of the Church and to have provided a rich theological teaching instruction and spiritual sustenance of the faithful. . . . In their explanations of the Bible, the Fathers mix and weave together typological and allegorical interpretations in a virtual inextricable way. But they do so always for a pastoral and pedagogical purpose, convinced that everything that has been written has been written for our instruction."[39]

94. To whom are Catholic Scripture scholars and exegetes (interpreters) answerable regarding their research and writings?

As stated in Art. 23 of *Dei Verbum*, they must work "under the watchful eye of the sacred Magisterium." As the *Catechism* teaches (No. 100): "The task of interpreting the Word of God authentically has been entrusted solely to the Magesterium of the Church, that is, to the pope and to the bishops in communion with him."

95. How does the study of Sacred Scripture relate to theology as a whole?

"The Sacred Scriptures . . . because they are inspired, are truly the Word of God. Therefore, *the study of the sacred page should be the very soul of sacred theology* . . . [P]astoral preaching, catechetics, and all forms of Christian instruction— among which the liturgical homily should hold pride of place"—are "healthily nourished and thrive in holiness through the Word of Scripture" (*DV* 24; emphasis added).

In his encyclical letter, *Divino Afflante Spiritu*, Pope Pius XII instructed biblical scholars to "set forth in particular the theological doctrine in faith and morals of the individual books or texts so that their exposition may not only aid the professors of theology in their explanations and proofs of the dogmas of the Faith, but may also be of assistance to priests in their presentation of Christian doctrine to the people, and in fine may help all the faithful to lead a life that is holy and worthy of a Christian" (Par. 24).

---

39. *Origins*, Jan. 6, 1994, *op. cit.*, pp 515–16.

The 1993 Pontifical Biblical Commission document, *The Interpretation of the Bible in the Church*, elaborates further on this point, saying that "exegetes must orient their research in such a fashion that 'the study of Sacred Scripture' can be in reality 'as it were the soul of theology.'" In regard to moral theology in particular, the commission made the point that "often the biblical texts are not concerned to distinguish universal moral principles from particular prescriptions of ritual purity and legal ordinances. All is mixed together."

On the other hand, the Bible reflects a considerable moral development, which finds its completion in the New Testament. It is not sufficient therefore that the Old Testament should indicate a certain moral position (e.g., the practice of slavery or of divorce, or that of extermination in the case of war) for this position to continue to have validity. One has to undertake a process of discernment. This will review the issue in light of the progress in moral understanding and sensitivity that has occurred over the years."[40]

96. Who should study Sacred Scripture?

"All clerics, particularly priests of Christ and others who, as deacons or catechists, are officially engaged in the ministry of the Word, *should immerse themselves in the Scriptures by constant sacred reading and diligent study.* . . . Likewise, the sacred Synod forcefully and specifically exhorts *all the Christian faithful* . . . to learn the 'surpassing knowledge of Jesus Christ' (Phil 3:8) by *frequent reading of the divine Scriptures.* For [as St. Jerome so wisely noted], 'ignorance of Scripture is ignorance of Christ'" (emphasis added; cf. *DV* 25)

In regard to the lay faithful, the Pontifical Biblical Commission offers these words: "The Spirit is, assuredly, also given to *individual Christians* . . . as they pray and prayerfully study the Scriptures within the context of their own personal lives. This is why the Second Vatican Council insisted that access to Scripture be facilitated in every possible way. . . . This kind of reading, it should be noted, is never completely private, for the believer always reads and interprets Scripture

---

40. *Ibid.,* p. 519.

within the faith of the Church and then brings back to the community the fruit of that reading for the enrichment of the common faith."[41]

97. What does the Council say must accompany the reading of Scripture?

"Prayer should accompany the reading of Sacred Scripture, so that a dialogue takes place between God and man. For [as St. Ambrose said], 'we speak to him when we pray; we listen to Him when we read the divine oracles'" (*DV* 25).

98. Who has the duty of instructing the faithful as to the correct use of Sacred Scripture?

The bishops, "with whom the apostolic doctrine resides", are responsible for this instruction (*DV* 25).

99. How are the bishops to do this?

" . . . by giving them [the faithful] translations of the sacred texts which are equipped with necessary and really adequate explanations" (*DV* 25).

100. How are the Eucharist and Sacred Scripture related?

"Just as from constant attendance at the eucharistic mystery the life of the Church draws increase, so a new impulse of spiritual life may be expected from increased veneration of the Word of God, which 'stands forever'" (*DV* 26; *Isa* 40:8; cf. *1 Pet* 1:23–25)."

---

41. *Ibid.*, p. 517.

Index

Numbers refer to questions, not pages